Painting and Decorating

CONSTRUCTION SERIES

Painting and Decorating

CONSTRUCTION SERIES

www.skills2learn.com
Experts in e-learning & virtual reality simulation

Australia • Brazil • Japan • Korea • Mexico • Singapore • Spain • United Kingdom • United States

Painting and Decorating
Skills2Learn

Publishing Director: Linden Harris

Commissioning Editor: Lucy Mills

Development Editor: Helen Green

Editorial Assistant: Claire Napoli

Project Editor: Lucy Arthy

Production Controller: Eyvett Davis

Marketing Manager: Jason Bennett

Typesetter: MPS Limited, a Macmillan Company

Cover design: HCT Creative

Text design: Design Deluxe

For product information and technology assistance,
contact **emea.info@cengage.com**.

For permission to use material from this text or product,
and for permission queries,
email **emea.permissions@cengage.com**.

DISCLAIMER

British Library Cataloguing-in-Publication Data

A catalogue record for this book is available from the British Library.

ISBN: 978-1-4080-4188-8

Cengage Learning EMEA

Cheriton House, North Way, Andover, Hampshire, SP10 5BE
United Kingdom

Cengage Learning products are represented in Canada by Nelson Education Ltd.

For your lifelong learning solutions, visit **www.cengage.co.uk**

Purchase your next print book, e-book or e-chapter at **www.cengagebrain.com**

Printed in Malta by Melita Press
1 2 3 4 5 6 7 8 9 10 – 14 13 12

2005711
£19.99

Contents

Foreword

The construction industry is a significant part of the UK economy and a major employer of people. It has a huge impact on the environment and plays a role in our everyday life in some shape or form. With environmental issues such as climate change and sustainable sourcing of materials now playing an important part in the design and construction of buildings and other structures, there is a need to educate and re-educate those new to the industry and those currently involved.

This construction series of e-learning programmes and text workbooks has been developed to provide a structured blended learning approach that will enhance the learning experience and stimulate a deeper understanding of the construction trades and give an awareness of sustainability issues. The content within these learning materials has been aligned to units of the Decorative Finishing and Industrial Painting, National Occupational Standards and can be used as a support tool whilst studying for any relevant vocational qualifications.

The uniqueness of this construction series is that it aims to bridge the gap between classroom-based and practical-based learning. The workbooks provide classroom-based activities that can involve learners in discussions and research tasks as well as providing them with understanding and knowledge of the subject. The e-learning programmes take the subject further, with high quality images, animations and audio further enhancing the content and showing information in a different light. In addition, the e-practical side of the e-learning places the learner in a virtual environment where they can move around freely, interact with objects and use the knowledge and skills they have gained from the workbook and e-learning to complete a set of tasks whilst in the comfort of a safe working environment.

The workbooks and e-learning programmes are designed to help learners continuously improve their skills and provide confidence and a sound knowledge base before getting their hands dirty in the real world.

About the Construction Consortia

This series of construction workbooks and e-learning programmes has been developed by the E-Construction Consortium. The consortium is a group of colleges and organizations that are passionate about the construction industry and are determined to enhance the learning experiences of people within the different trades or those that are new to it.

The consortium members have many years experience in the construction and educational sectors and have created this blended learning approach of interactive e-learning programmes and text workbooks to achieve the aim of:

- Providing accessible training in different areas of construction.
- Bridging the gap between classroom-based and practical-based learning.
- Providing a concentrated set of improvement learning modules.
- Enabling learners to gain new skills and qualifications more effectively.
- Improving functional skills and awareness of sustainability issues within the industry.
- Promoting health and safety in the industry.
- Encouraging training and continuous professional development.

For more information about this construction series please visit: **www.e-construction.co.uk** or **www.skills2learn.com**.

About e-learning

INTRODUCTION

This construction series of workbooks and e-learning programmes uses a blended learning approach to train learners about construction skills. Blended learning allows training to be delivered through different mediums such as books, e-learning (computer-based training), practical workshops and traditional classroom techniques. These training methods are designed to complement each other and work in tandem to achieve overall learning objectives and outcomes.

E-LEARNING

The Painting and Decorating e-learning programme that is also available to sit alongside this workbook offers a different method of learning. With technology playing an increasingly important part of everyday life, e-learning uses visually rich 2D and 3D graphics/animation, audio, video, text and interactive quizzes, to allow you to engage with the content and learn at your own pace and in your own time.

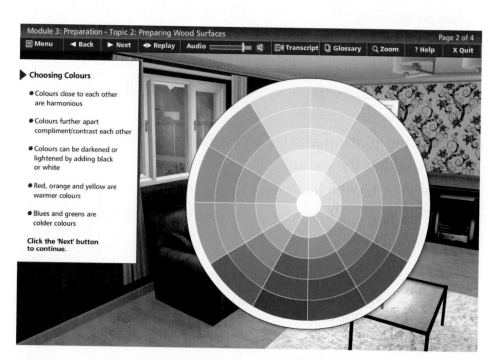

E-PRACTICAL

Part of the e-learning programme is an e-practical interactive scenario. This facility allows you to be immersed in a virtual reality situation where the choices you make affect the outcome. Using 3D technology, you can move freely around the environment, interact with objects, carry out tests, and make decisions and mistakes until you have mastered the subject. By practising in a virtual environment you will not only be able to see what you've learnt but also analyze your approach and thought process to the problem.

BENEFITS OF E-LEARNING

Diversity – E-learning can be used for almost anything. With the correct approach any subject can be brought to life to provide an interactive training experience.

Technology – Advancements in computer technology now allow a wide range of spectacular and engaging e-learning to be delivered to a wider population.

Captivate and Motivate – Hold the learner's attention for longer with the use of high quality graphics, animation, sound and interactivity.

Safe Environment – E-practical scenarios can create environments which simulate potentially harmful real-life situations or replicate a piece of dangerous equipment, therefore allowing the learner to train and gain experience and knowledge in a completely safe environment.

Instant Feedback – Learners can undertake training assessments that feed back results instantly. This can provide information on where they need to re-study or congratulate them on passing the assessment. Results and certificates can also be printed for future records.

On-Demand – Can be accessed 24 hours a day, 7 days a week, 365 days of the year. You can access the content at any time and view it at your own pace.

Portable Solutions – Can be delivered via a CD, website or LMS. Learners no longer need to travel to all lectures, conferences, meetings or training days. This saves many man-hours in reduced travelling, cost of hotels and expenses amongst other things.

Reduction of Costs – Can be used to teach best practice processes on jobs which use large quantities or expensive materials. Learners can practise their techniques and boost their confidence to a high enough standard before being allowed near real materials.

PAINTING AND DECORATING E-LEARNING

The aim of the painting and decorating e-learning programme is to enhance a learner's knowledge and understanding of the painting and decorating trade. The course content is aligned to units from the Decorative Finishing and Industrial Painting: National Occupational Standards (NOS) so can be used for study towards certification.

The programme gives the learners an understanding of the technicalities of painting and decorating as well as looking at sustainability, health and safety and functional skills in an interactive and visually engaging manner. It also provides a 'real-life' scenario where the learner can apply the knowledge gained from the tutorials in a safe yet practical way.

By using and completing this programme, it is expected that learners will:

- Understand the role of the painter/decorator in the working environment and have knowledge of some of the tools that will be used.
- Be able to explain the choice of materials for a project, calculate the correct quantities, source these from an appropriate supplier and identify the correct disposal method for waste materials.
- Understand the preparation required for painting and wall-papering different surfaces.
- Know how to apply paint and wallpaper to different surfaces and know techniques for different situations.

The e-learning programme is divided into the following learning modules:

- Getting Started
- Tools and Materials
- Preparation
- Painting
- Hanging Wallcoverings
- End Test
- Interactive E-Practical Scenario

THE CONSTRUCTION SERIES

As part of the construction series the following e-learning programmes and workbooks are available. For more information please contact the sales team on **emea.fesales@cengage.com** or visit the website **www.e-construction.co.uk**.

- Plastering
- Bricklaying
- Carpentry & Joinery
- Painting & Decorating
- Wall & Floor Tiling

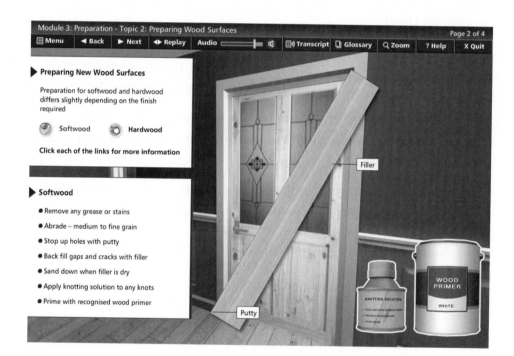

About the NOS

The National Occupational Standards (NOS) provide a framework of information that outline the skills, knowledge and understanding required to carry out work-based activities within a given vocation. Each standard is divided into units that cover specific activities of that occupation. Employers, employees, teachers and learners can use these standards as an information, support and reference resource that will enable them to understand the skills and criteria required for good practice in the workplace.

The standards are used as a basis to develop many vocational qualifications in the United Kingdom for a wide range of occupations. This workbook and associated e-learning programme are aligned to the Decorative Finishing and Industrial Painting, National Occupational Standards, and the information within relates to the following units:

- Conform to General Workplace Safety
- Move and Handle Resources
- Confirm Work Activities and Resources for Work
- Develop and Maintain Good Working Relationships
- Prepare New Surfaces for Paint Systems
- Prepare Surfaces for Painting and Decorating
- Apply Paint Systems by Brush and Roller
- Hang Wallcoverings (Standard Papers)

About the book

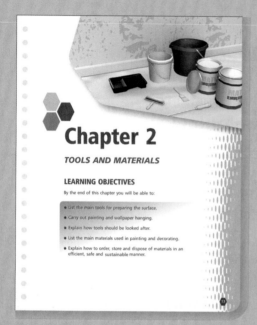

Learning Objectives at the start of each chapter explain the skills and knowledge you need to be proficient in and understand by the end of the chapter.

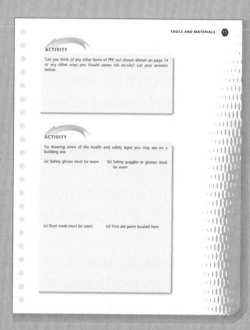

Activities are practical tasks that engage you in the subject and further your understanding.

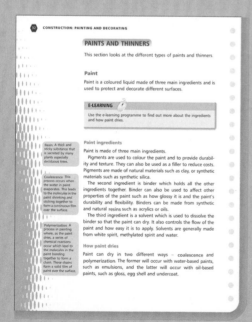

E-Learning Icons link the workbook content to the e-learning programme.

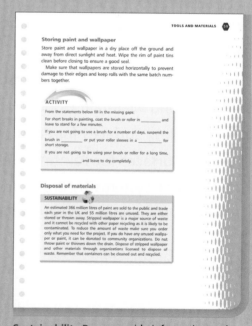

Sustainability Boxes provide information and helpful advice on how to work in a sustainable and environmentally friendly way.

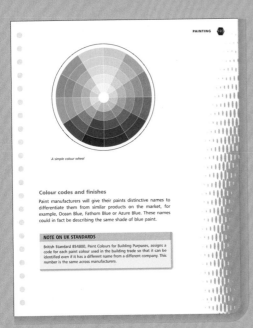

Note on UK Standards draws your attention to relevant building regulations.

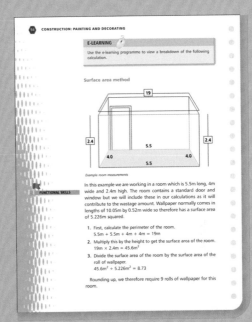

Functional Skills Icons highlight activities that develop and test your Maths, English and ICT key skills.

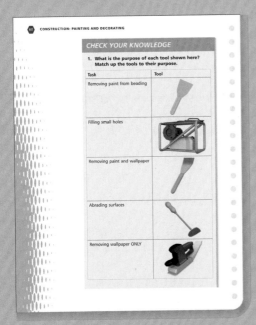

Check Your Knowledge at the end of each chapter to test your knowledge and understanding.

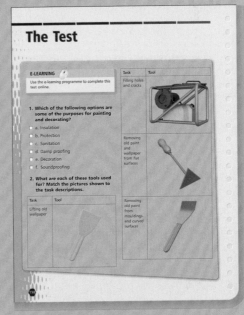

End Test in Chapter 6 checks your knowledge on all the information within the workbook.

Chapter 1

GETTING STARTED

LEARNING OBJECTIVES

By the end of this chapter you will be able to:

- List the main purposes for painting and decorating.

- Explain the skills required to be a painter and decorator.

- Explain who you will be communicating with on-site and why.

NOS REFERENCE

Confirm Work Activities and Resources for Work

Develop and Maintain Good Working Relationships

INTRODUCTION

The purpose of painting and decorating

Painting and decorating a building can satisfy one or more of the following purposes.

Sanitation

Buildings such as hospitals and canteens need to have surfaces that can easily be cleaned to avoid the build-up of contamination, mould and fungi.

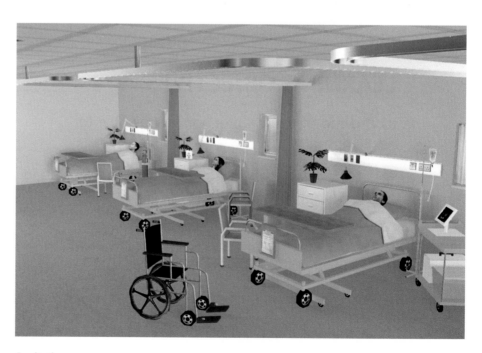

Sanitation

Conservation

Buildings can be conserved using various paints, coverings and techniques. Older buildings will need careful work to ensure they are maintained or in some circumstances restored to their original condition. This can involve using traditional paints such as **lime** wash which are sympathetic to the appearance and character of the original building.

Lime There are two types of lime, hydraulic and non-hydraulic. They can both be used for mortar and pointing. The difference is in the setting time. The ratio for a lime mortar mix is six parts sand, one part lime and one part cement. Production and sustainability benefits make lime an eco-friendly material.

Conservation

Protection

Exterior and interior surfaces need to be protected against weather conditions, wear and tear, and damage. Paints can be applied to external surfaces to protect against the elements and to areas with high traffic such as corridors in schools. These can be protected by hard-wearing wallcoverings and paints.

Protection

Decoration

Painting and decorating can provide decoration to a building as well as protection. A range of colours and finishes are available as well as different wallcoverings to suit most tastes. Stains and varnishes can be used to enhance the appearance of wood.

Decoration

Identification

Painting and decorating can be used for identification purposes, for example by using different coloured zones in large buildings to help visitors find their way around, and to help engineers identify the contents of different piping (although this can also be done by adding labels to the pipes).

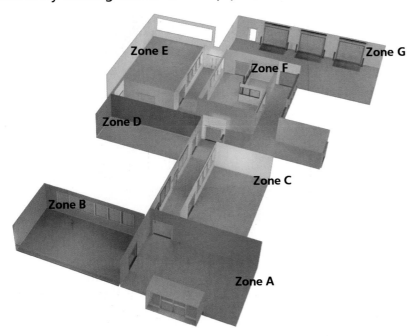

Zone E

Zone G

Zone F

Zone D

Zone C

Zone B

Zone A

Identification of different areas

ACTIVITY

For the list of purposes below, give some examples of places where these needs exist.

Sanitation	
Conservation	
Protection	
Decoration	
Identification	

The role of the painter and decorator

As a painter and decorator you will be responsible for preparing and decorating a surface in response to your client's requirements. The jobs you will be doing will depend upon the area you work in.

You might work for a large construction firm where you will be part of a team preparing and painting the interior of buildings and offices. Alternatively, you may work for a smaller firm or be self-employed where you could work on your own, painting and decorating private houses and other local work. The skills for a painter and decorator are the same whichever area you work in.

Skills required by a tiler

JOB VACANCY

Job Title:
Painter/Decorator

Location:
Nationwide

Hours:
Average 37.5 hours per week

Work Pattern:
Monday to Friday

Skills Required:
● Punctual and reliable
● Work to a high standard
● Respect the area of work
● Work hard and effectively
● Good eye for detail
● Good colour vision
● Excellent practical skills
● Awareness of Health and Safety issues
● Work alone or as part of a larger team

ACTIVITY

List below what skills are needed to be a painter and decorator. Look through your local paper or search the internet to find job vacancies for painters and decorators and see what skills they are advertising for.

The painter and decorator on-site

The painter and decorator will usually arrive towards the end of any project. The painter and decorator's job is to:

- Measure the surfaces to work out how much paint or wall-coverings is required.
- Liaise with the client over the choice of paints, materials and colours.
- Prepare the working area removing or protecting objects as required.
- Prepare the surfaces including stripping old wallcoverings or paint and filling any cracks or holes.
- Mix the paints either by hand or with a computer colour matching system.
- Apply the paint to the surfaces and hang the wallcoverings.
- Clean and tidy up afterwards.

Painting and decorating involves a number of tasks

ACTIVITY

Are there any other jobs that you think a painter and decorator could be involved in when on-site? List any you think of below.

COMMUNICATION

Building design

Each building job will have a design specification document and a bill of quantities. These documents will contain:

- Detailed plans of the build.
- Information on how the construction should be built.
- A list of materials that need to be used and their quantities.

NOTE ON UK STANDARDS

These documents will be required to satisfy and comply with Building Regulations and meet the approval of local authorities. You will need to refer to and understand these documents to make sure the building is constructed correctly.

Design specifications and bill of quantities

E-LEARNING

Use the e-learning programme to see more building design documents.

ACTIVITY

Why do you think the building design document is important? List your ideas below.

Working together

Although the decorator is not required on-site until the second fix stage of the construction process, communication with other trades is very important.

You might need to talk with the architect, client or site foreman about the specific details of the project. You will need to know what surfaces you will be decorating, whether there will be any special features that are required, what sort of materials will be needed, and you will need to order the materials.

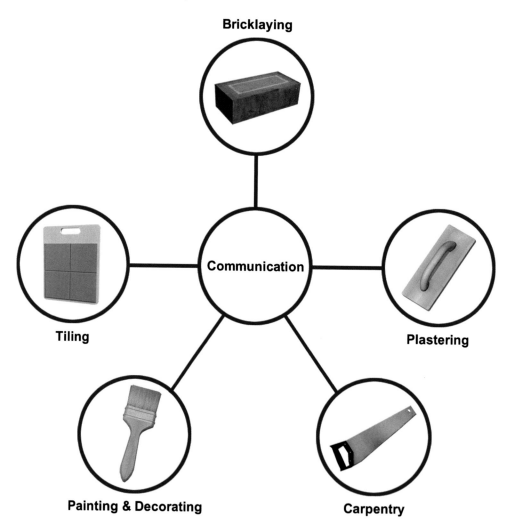

Communicating with other people

You will also need to discuss the logistics of the project, for example when will you be able to start work, how soon does the work need to be completed, how will you gain access to the site, where you can store your materials, and how you can dispose of materials.

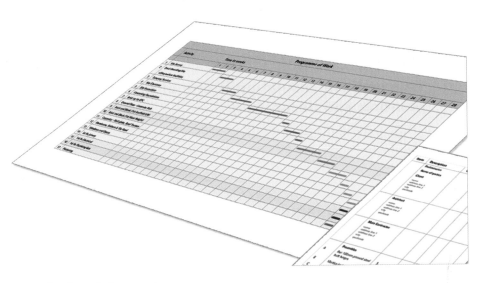

Example of work documents

ACTIVITY

List below any other trades or people you may need to talk to when carrying out a job.

CHECK YOUR KNOWLEDGE

1. **True or False: Insulation is one of the purposes for painting and decorating.**

   ☐ a. True

   ☐ b. False

2. **Select which requirement from the list is INCORRECT. To be a painter and decorator you need to:**

   ☐ a. Be punctual and reliable

   ☐ b. Work to a high standard

   ☐ c. Be over 21

   ☐ d. Respect your working area especially if it is a private home

   ☐ e. Have a good eye for detail and good colour vision

   ☐ f. Have excellent practical skills

   ☐ g. Be able to work on your own or as part of a team

   ☐ h. Have a sound awareness of Health and Safety issues

3. **True or False: The painter and decorator will usually arrive at the start of a project.**

   ☐ a. True

   ☐ b. False

Chapter 2

TOOLS AND MATERIALS

LEARNING OBJECTIVES

By the end of this chapter you will be able to:

- List the main tools for preparing the surface.

- Carry out painting and wallpaper hanging.

- Explain how tools should be looked after.

- List the main materials used in painting and decorating.

- Explain how to order, store and dispose of materials in an efficient, safe and sustainable manner.

Sustainable materials Materials that have been sourced by causing little or no damage to the environment.

NOS REFERENCE

Conform to General Workplace Safety

Move and Handle Resources

Confirm Work Activities and Resources for Work

INTRODUCTION

Using tools safely

You should use tools only for their proper purpose and make sure you follow all instructions. You should always wear the appropriate **personal protective equipment (PPE)**.

Personal Protective Equipment (PPE) Depending on the type of work, there are different types of equipment specifically designed to protect your health and safety. Examples include gloves, safety boots, goggles and dust mask.

HEALTH & SAFETY

- Only use equipment you have been trained to use.
- Always clean the equipment after use.
- Test electrical equipment regularly.
- Do not use equipment that appears to be damaged.
- Do not use items if the date of the last check has expired.

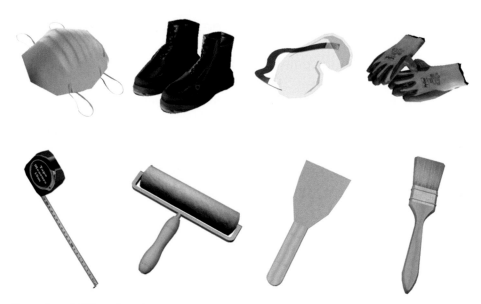

Examples of PPE and tools

ACTIVITY

Can you think of any other items of PPE not shown shown on page 14 or any other ways you should assess risk on-site? List your answers below.

ACTIVITY

Try drawing some of the health and safety signs you may see on a building site.

(a) Safety gloves must be worn

(b) Safety goggles or glasses must be worn

(c) Dust mask must be worn

(d) First aid point located here

TOOLS AND EQUIPMENT

Removing old paint and wallcoverings

Before you start applying paint or a new wallcovering, you will need to prepare the surface. This may involve removing old paint or wallcoverings. Tools to remove old paint and wallcoverings include paint scrapers and shave hooks, hot air guns and steam strippers to remove wallpaper. Old wallcoverings must be removed from surfaces before re-papering, otherwise the new covering will not hold.

Removing surface coverings can involve a number of tasks

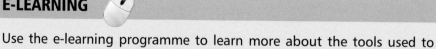

E-LEARNING

Use the e-learning programme to learn more about the tools used to remove old paint and wallcoverings.

Paint scrapers

Paint scrapers are used to remove old paint and wallpaper. Sizes of the blade vary from 25mm to 100mm.

Paint scraper

Shave hooks

Shave hooks are used in conjunction with heat guns to strip paint and varnish from moulded woodwork. You should make sure that the blade is kept sharp. There are three different shapes; the pear, triangular and combination hooks for different shaped surfaces.

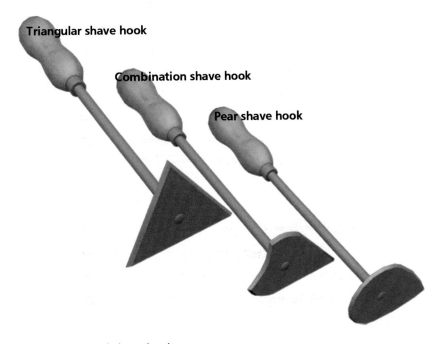

Triangular shave hook

Combination shave hook

Pear shave hook

Different shaped shave hooks

Hot air guns

Hot air guns apply heated air to soften paint and varnish so that they can be removed with shave hooks and scrapers. Electric hot air guns are mainly used, although gas heat guns are an alternative. They have the advantage that they do not scorch the woodwork. Hot air guns have different shaped nozzles to direct the heat.

Hot air gun

Steam strippers

Steam strippers apply steam to the surface of wallpaper to soften it for removal. They work by heating water to produce steam and piping the steam through to a flat plate which is held against the paper. The steam impregnates the wallpaper and loosens the **adhesive** so that you can remove the paper with a scraper.

Adhesive General term given to a range of bonding agents.

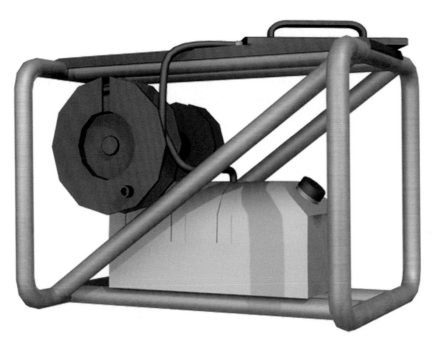

Steam stripper

HEALTH & SAFETY

Take extra care when using equipment that generates heat and steam and make sure they have cooled completely before storing away.

ACTIVITY

Where are these pieces of equipment used? List your ideas below.

Paint scrapers	
Shave hooks	
Hot air guns	
Steam strippers	

Preparing surfaces

You will need to use a number of tools to prepare the surface before applying new paint or wallcovering. This will include sanders to smooth the surface down and filling knives to fill holes and indentations.

Good preparation is vital

E-LEARNING

Use the e-learning programme to learn more about the tools used for preparing surfaces.

Filling knife

A filling knife has a flexible blade and is used to apply filler to holes, indentations and cracks in the surface. The blade size can vary from 25mm to 150mm.

Filling knife

Electric sander

Electric sanders are used to sand down surfaces before painting or hanging wallpapers. When using a sander, make sure you keep it moving and replace the sandpaper from coarse to fine grade to get the required finish.

Sanders use three basic motions: orbital, where the sanding plate moves in small circles, belt, where the sander moves in one direction only and rotary, where the entire sanding plate rotates.

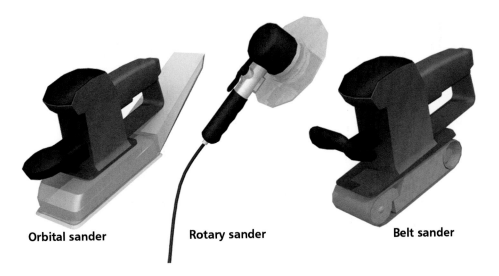

Orbital sander   **Rotary sander**   **Belt sander**

Different types of sander

Paintbrushes

Brushes are used to apply paint and adhesives to different surfaces. They come in a range of sizes from 12mm (half an inch) to 175mm (7 inches) and are made up of three components.

The handle is usually made of seasoned wood or plastic. Make sure that it is comfortable to hold.

The filling can be made from natural or man-made fibres such as wild boar bristle or nylon, or a mixture. The choice of fibre will depend upon the type of work. Nylon fibres are typically used to apply water-based paints.

The ferrule is the metal part between the handle and the filling. It can be made from nickel plated steel or copper.

When choosing a brush, check the density and length of the filling and that it is securely held in the ferrule.

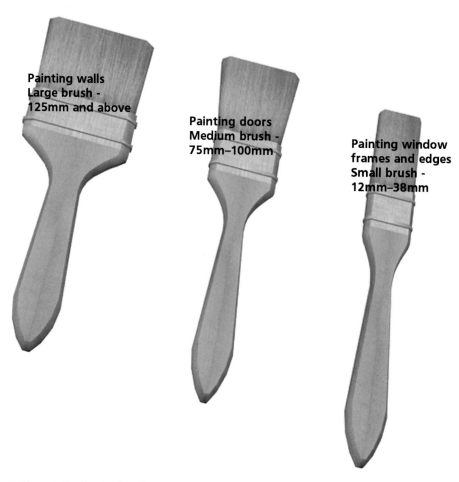

Painting walls
Large brush -
125mm and above

Painting doors
Medium brush -
75mm–100mm

Painting window
frames and edges
Small brush -
12mm–38mm

Different sized paint brushes

ACTIVITY

The image shows a room that needs painting. Match up the different brushes with the different tasks and label the image with the correct answers.

Small brush	Painting doors
Medium brush	Painting walls
Large brush	Painting around edges (cutting in)

ACTIVITY

This is a typical paintbrush, identify and label the three component parts.

Rollers

Rollers are used for covering larger areas. You will need to use a brush to fill in around the edges. Rollers can be single or double armed. Single armed rollers are used for domestic work whilst double arm rollers are used to cover larger areas. Both types of roller can have extension arms attached to reach higher areas. Other rollers are designed for specific purposes, for example radiator rollers used for painting or wallpapering behind radiators without the need to remove them.

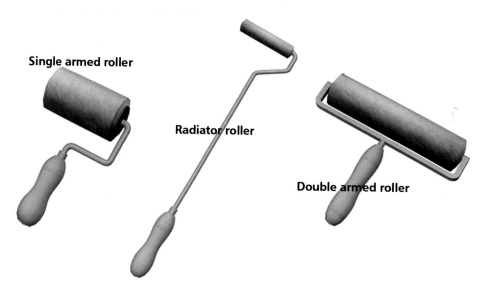

Single armed roller

Radiator roller

Double armed roller

Different types of roller

Roller sleeves and pile

Roller sleeves can also come in different lengths of pile: short, medium, or heavy pile and are made from different materials.

- Short pile – made from sponge, foam, or mohair.
- Medium pile – made from lamb's wool or synthetic fibre.
- Heavy pile – made from synthetic fibre.

Make sure that you use the correct pile for the material used as the wrong pile will result in poor application.

ACTIVITY

What type of roller pile do you think should be used for the following types of paint? Complete the table below.

Paint	Type of pile (short, medium, heavy)
Gloss	
Emulsion	
Egg shell	
Exterior surfaces	
Undercoat	
Textured surfaces	

Specialist equipment

As well as the traditional methods of painting with brushes and rollers, there is also specialist equipment available. These can range from the more professional to simple DIY tools. Some of the more specialist tools can be quite expensive.

E-LEARNING

Use the e-learning programme to learn more about specialist equipment.

HVLP spray systems

HVLP is a spray method where the paint is atomized by high volume, low pressure air. The paint supply is usually attached to the HVLP spray gun, or contained in a remote pressure tank connected to the spray gun via a hose. Using a HVLP system gives you a good level of control and reduces overspray. A HVLP system is good for small internal areas or for use on wood and furniture.

Airless systems

An airless spray system can be used for all manner of jobs including large-scale buildings. It pumps the paint out of a spray gun at high pressure and can cover a large area quickly. This method is also good for applying a high build coat with a thick film.

HEALTH & SAFETY

When spraying you should always wear the correct PPE and work in a well ventilated environment.

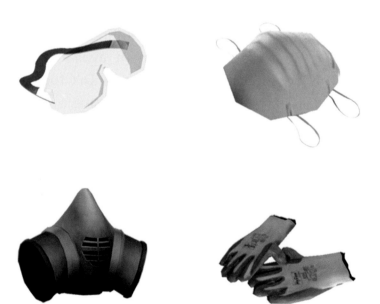

Selection of PPE that can be used when spray painting

DIY tools

Alternative methods which can be cheaper include paint pod systems where you can control the flow of paint. This allows good coverage and is easy to use.

A paint pad can be used in a number of locations and is an alternative to a conventional brush or roller. They generally provide a smooth finish with very little splash marks. They can be ideal for corners or painting round fittings and can be reasonably priced.

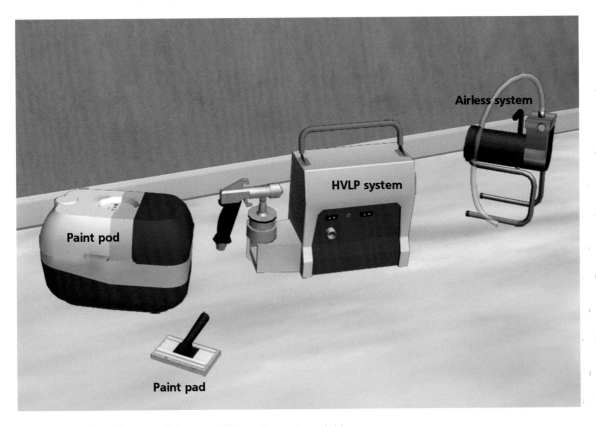

A representation of some of the specialist equipment available

ACTIVITY

Hidden in the wordsearch are the following 11 words associated with tools. The words may be written forwards, backwards, up, down or diagonally. Draw a ring around the words once you have found them.

```
M L S N U G R I A T O H Z C M M G
U O J M J Z N Q G M V V U Z L S X
S R E P P I R T S M A E T S M E A
A S T J U C M C S N E W E L S I
U K L R C S H E F L F Q T E J R R
X O Y A I T E X O I Q S C D M E L
L O Z D I G L X N T Y T W Q S P E
Q H T R E Z K K S S R X G L D A S
Z E B W V A G C Y I N I O R A R S
E V F D Y N J A C I P O A R Y C S
F A F C I S R S I W T Y H H N S Y
A H M L M P A L I Y V Q B M A T S
X S L N S N Y D I F K P J B U N T
N I V P D U O D O T M M D W M I E
F H L E E M U Y S R E L L O R A M
A V R C T B U M W W Z I I O W P S
H S E H S U R B T N I A P Z D F I
```

AIRLESS SYSTEMS, PAINTBRUSHES, DIY TOOLS, PAINT SCRAPERS, ELECTRIC SANDER, ROLLERS, FILLING KNIFE, SHAVE HOOKS, HOT AIR GUNS, STEAM STRIPPERS, HVLP SPRAY SYSTEMS

Tools for hanging wallpaper

Hanging wallpaper involves measuring up to ensure that you have the appropriate amount of paper, setting out on the wall so that the paper is hung square, cutting the paper to size, pasting and hanging the paper and finally trimming strips around the edges. You will need a number of tools to carry out these tasks.

E-LEARNING

Use the e-learning programme to learn more about tools for hanging wallpaper.

Measuring and setting out

You will need to use tape measures, straight edges, **plumb bobs** and **spirit levels** to ensure the paper is hung vertical.

> **Plumb bob** A weight attached to the plumb line, for checking vertical lines.

> **Spirit level** A tool used to check true vertical and horizontal lines indicated by a bubble in spirit-filled vials.

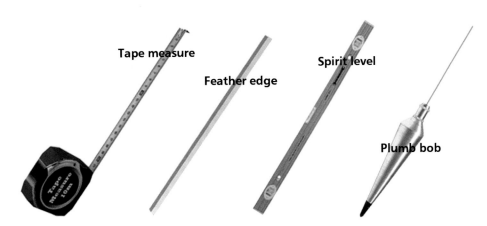

Tape measure

Feather edge

Spirit level

Plumb bob

Selection of tools for setting out

Cutting paper to size

Shears or scissors are the most common tools used for cutting paper. Trimming knives are used to cut around electric sockets and similar obstacles after the paper has been hung. A trimming knife can be used with a straight edge. Make sure the blades of all cutting devices are protected and clean and free from adhesive.

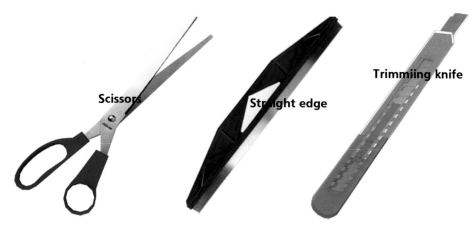

Selection of tools for cutting

Pasting and hanging paper

Paste brushes typically have shorter bristles to distribute the adhesive more evenly. Widths of the brushes would normally be from 100mm to 175mm. Wash paste brushes out immediately after use. Paste tables are typically wooden folding leaves of around 2m long by around 0.5m wide.

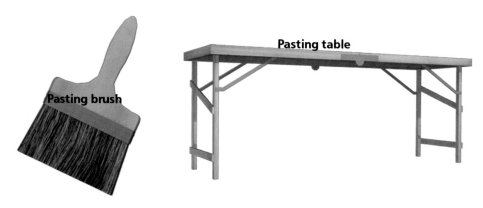

Selection of tools for pasting

ACTIVITY

In the table below state all the tools you can think of that are needed for the following tasks:

Task	Tools
Measuring and setting out	
Cutting paper to size	
Pasting and hanging paper	

ACTIVITY

Label each of the tools shown.

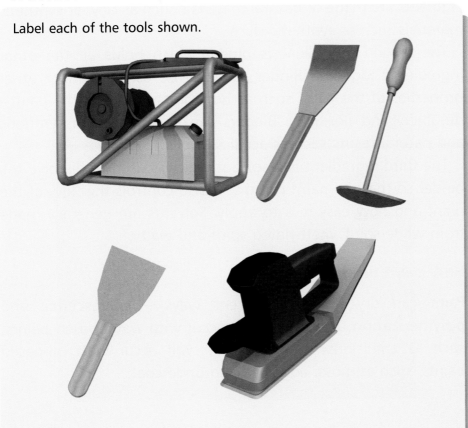

PAINTS AND THINNERS

This section looks at the different types of paints and thinners.

Paint

Paint is a coloured liquid made of three main ingredients and is used to protect and decorate different surfaces.

E-LEARNING

Use the e-learning programme to find out more about the ingredients and how paint dries.

Resin A thick and sticky substance that is secreted by many plants especially deciduous trees.

Coalescence This process occurs when the water in paint evaporates. This leads to the molecules in the paint shrinking and sticking together to form a continuous film over the surface.

Polymerization A process in painting where, as the paint dries, a series of chemical reactions occur which lead to the molecules in the paint bonding together to form a chain. These chains form a solid film of paint over the surface.

Paint ingredients

Paint is made of three main ingredients.

Pigments are used to colour the paint and to provide durability and texture. They can also be used as a filler to reduce costs. Pigments are made of natural materials such as clay, or synthetic materials such as synthetic silica.

The second ingredient is binder which holds all the other ingredients together. Binder can also be used to affect other properties of the paint such as how glossy it is and the paint's durability and flexibility. Binders can be made from synthetic and natural **resins** such as acrylics or oils.

The third ingredient is a solvent which is used to dissolve the binder so that the paint can dry. It also controls the flow of the paint and how easy it is to apply. Solvents are generally made from white spirit, methylated spirit and water.

How paint dries

Paint can dry in two different ways – **coalescence** and **polymerization**. The former will occur with water-based paints, such as emulsions, and the latter will occur with oil-based paints, such as gloss, egg shell and undercoat.

Paint systems

E-LEARNING

Use the e-learning programme to find out more about the different paint systems.

Paints are usually applied in a combination of coats to provide protection and decoration to surfaces. This is known as a paint system.

There are a number of things you will need to consider when choosing a paint system for your project. These include the type and condition of the surface, the compatibility of the elements of the paint system, and the drying time for each of the coats. The type of paint system required will be specified in the project details or in consultation with the client.

Consider the current conditions and location before starting

A paint system can be one or more coats depending upon the type of paint and the surface to be covered. A typical three coat system could consist of a primer, an undercoat and a topcoat.

Primer

The primer is used as a preparatory coat before applying the paint. It seals the surface, provides additional protection and forms a key to help the paint stick.

Undercoat

An undercoat is applied to exterior or interior primed surfaces. It is a heavy bodied layer of paint which provides film thickness, opacity and filling properties.

Topcoat

The topcoat provides the finishing coat and the final colour. Its job is to provide a protective layer which resists everyday wear and tear as well as atmospheric conditions. It should provide a wipe clean finish.

ACTIVITY

Label the figure to identify each coat of a three coat system.

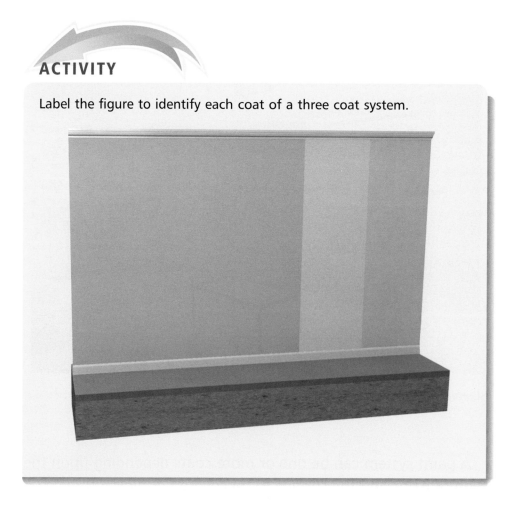

Types of paints

E-LEARNING

Use the e-learning programme to find out more about the different types of paints.

There are three main types of paints available.

Solvent borne

Solvent borne paints include gloss and semi-gloss or egg shell finishes. They can be used on most materials but are particularly good for surfaces covered in old paint. Solvent borne paints tend to need a little more care with application. The drying time is typically 8 to 24 hours. Brushes will need to be cleaned in white spirit afterwards.

Water-based

Water-based paints such as emulsion and acrylic are used on wood, concrete, masonry and brick. They can usually be applied smoothly but may need additional coats. They will take around 1 to 6 hours to dry and brushes can be washed out in water.

Varnishes

Varnishes are typically used on wood and tend to be clear. They can be either solvent borne or water-based. They are used to enhance the appearance of the wood as well as to protect it.

Solvent borne   Water-based   Varnishes

The three main types of paints

ACTIVITY

For each of the paints listed state whether the paint is solvent borne, water-based or a varnish and where it could be used.

Paint	Type of paint	Where to be used
Egg shell		
Emulsion		
Matt		
Acrylic		
Gloss		

Ordering paint

E-LEARNING

Use the e-learning programme to see how you can calculate the amount of paint needed for a room.

When painting a room it is important to order the correct amount to save on materials and costs. You will need to take into consideration the surface to be painted, the amount of coats needed and the type of paint used.

Planning the amount of paint required is essential

In this example we are working in a room with smooth, previously painted surfaces which are 5.5m long, 4m wide and 2.4m high. The room contains a standard door and window but we will include these in our calculations as it will contribute to the wastage amount. We are going to be using an emulsion paint which has a spreading rate of approximately 12m^2 per litre.

FUNCTIONAL SKILLS

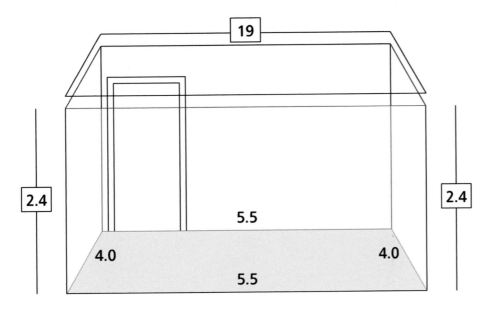

Work out the measurements of the area to be painted

Perimeter The border or outer boundary of an area.

1. First, calculate the **perimeter** of the room
   5.5m + 5.5m + 4m + 4m = 19m

2. Multiply the perimeter by the height to get the surface area of the room
   $19m \times 2.4m = 45.6m^2$

3. Divide the surface area by the spreading rate of the paint
   $45.6m^2 \div 12m^2 = 3.8$ litres

Rounding up, we therefore require 4 litres of paint for one coat of this room.

Remember to apply the correct number of coats to the surface

ACTIVITY

You are working in a room with smooth previously painted surfaces which are 7m long, 5m wide and 2.4m high. The room contains a standard door and window but include these in the calculations as it will contribute to the wastage amount. You are going to be using an emulsion paint which has a spreading rate of approximately 12m^2 per litre. Work out how many litres of paint will be required. Show your working out below.

Thinners

Most paints do not require thinning as this could result in a poor finish. If you do need to use a thinner then always follow the manufacturer's instructions and add thinner gradually until the appropriate consistency has been achieved. Thinners may be used to achieve the consistency needed for paint which is going to be sprayed, to revive old paints and to thin paint to allow penetration of particular surfaces to seal them. They can also be used to clean tools that have been used on the appropriate materials. Water-based paints may also be thinned to aid application.

Types of thinners include:

- methylated spirit
- white spirit
- water.

WALL HANGINGS AND ADHESIVES

This section looks at the different types of wall hangings and adhesives and ordering wallcoverings.

Lining papers

Lining paper is used to provide a surface with an even porosity and to hide any irregularities. Lining papers come in a variety of grades including 800 grade, which is used for walls and ceilings in standard condition, 1000 grade, a medium grade used on **plaster** walls and ceilings with minor imperfections, 1200 grade, a heavyweight grade for moderately rough surfaces, and 1400 grade, a super heavyweight grade which offers exceptional strength on rough surfaces.

You should hang lining paper vertically if you are going to paint the surface but hang it horizontally if you intend to cover it with wallpaper.

Plaster A white or pinkish mineral formed from heating gypsum at high temperatures. Plaster is used to protect and enhance the appearance of the surface as it provides a joint-less finish.

Vertical lining paper – painting

Horizontal lining paper – wallpaper

ACTIVITY

List some possible uses for the different grades of lining paper below.

Grade	Uses
800	
1000	
1400	
1800	

Decorative papers

There are different types of decorative papers. The choice of paper will depend upon the specifications for the project and the room to be covered.

E-LEARNING

Use the e-learning programme to learn more about the different types of decorative papers.

Ingrains

Ingrain papers are also known as woodchip. They are manufactured by placing small particles of wood or cork chippings between two layers of paper. Textures can be heavy or light. This type of paper is used to mask surface irregularities. A standard roll size is 0.52 or 0.53m wide and 10.05m long but double, triple and even quadruple rolls are also available.

Embossed

Embossed patterned papers can be plain or coloured and range from lightweight to heavyweight. They can also be used to mask surface irregularities and can be painted over. Take care not to brush out the embossed pattern when hanging.

Vinyl

Vinyl papers are made by bonding a vinyl sheet onto cotton or paper backing. Colours and designs are fused onto the vinyl during manufacture. They are fully washable and are not marked by mild soaps or detergents. When redecoration is required, unlike traditional papers which have to be stripped by a wet process, the vinyl top layer is peeled away from its backing leaving a lining base.

Relief vinyl

Relief vinyls are paper-backed vinyls, also known as blown vinyls. They can have thermal, soundproof and flameproof properties. Unlike vinyl paper, they have a permanent emboss which cannot be flattened when being applied.

Specialist

There are many other specialist types of wallpapers, some of which require special hanging techniques. These include flocks, foils, **hessians**, grass cloths, contract vinyls, handprints, **lincrusta** and photo murals.

Hessian A natural-looking wallpaper that has a textured feel. It can be made from fabric or a woven material.

Lincrusta A deeply embossed wall-covering.

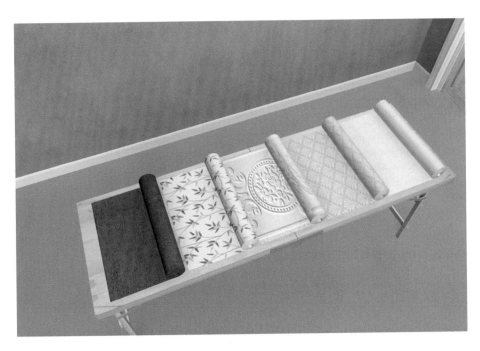

A range of wallpapers are available

ACTIVITY

Why might you choose to use the following types of wallpaper?

Type	Properties
Ingrains	
Embossed	
Vinyls	
Specialist	
Relief vinyls	

Matching patterned paper

E-LEARNING

Use the e-learning programme to learn more about the three ways that the pattern on wallpaper could match.

There are three ways that the pattern on wallpaper could match.

Random pattern

The first is a random pattern which will match no matter how the paper is hung and because there is no pattern to match there is generally less waste.

Random pattern

Set pattern

The set pattern is where the design elements match on adjoining strips. Each strip of paper will be the same at the ceiling line.

Set pattern

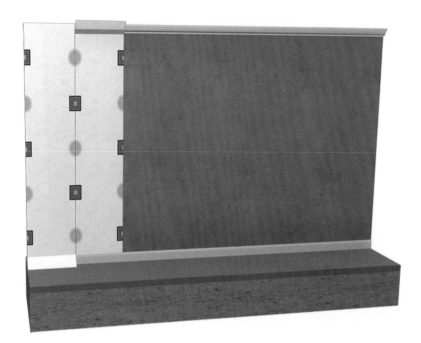

Drop match pattern

Drop match pattern

The drop match, or offset match pattern, is where the pattern runs diagonally across the wall. Always lay the wallpaper out first before cutting. Depending on the height of your wall, most wallpapers will have a three or four drop pattern. You will need to move each length up or down to make sure every other length will match at the ceiling line. The distance you will need to move each length will usually appear on the wallpaper label. This will have an impact upon the amount of paper you need to buy.

ACTIVITY

For the three symbols shown, identify which one represents random, set and drop match patterns?

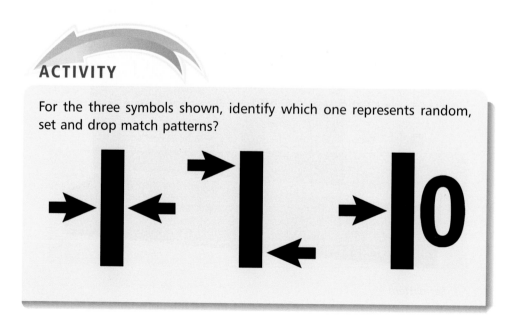

Handling adhesives

There are a number of things to remember when mixing or handling adhesives. Make sure all mixing utensils are clean before use and follow manufacturers' mixing instructions. Make sure there are no lumps in the adhesive when ready for use. Check previously used adhesive to make sure that it has not been contaminated. If it has been, discard it.

Take the necessary precautions with adhesives

HEALTH & SAFETY

Certain types of adhesives give off harmful vapours so make sure you wear the correct PPE.

ACTIVITY

What PPE should you use when working with adhesives? Tick the correct PPE:

Dust mask   Boots   Goggles   Gloves

Hard hat   Knee pads   High visibilty jacket   Ear defenders

Types of adhesives

There are a number of different adhesives used for different types of wall hangings. You must follow the manufacturers' instructions at all times.

E-LEARNING

Use the e-learning programme to learn more about the different types of adhesives.

Cellulose adhesive

Lightweight papers such as porous papers can be fixed with a cellulose adhesive. Wood or cotton cellulose is mixed with an alkali to form a solid powder which is then mixed with cold water. Cellulose adhesives have high water content and will not stick to heavier papers.

Cellulose adhesive

Starch based paste

Starch based paste is made from dry flakes of starch mixed with cold water. The ratio of water to flakes determines the strength of the paste. A guide to the ratios required for different surfaces can be found on the flake packaging. Starch based paste is used for medium weight papers.

Starch based paste

Vinyl adhesive

Vinyl adhesives can be used to stick light to heavy vinyl papers. Vinyl adhesives can be made from clay or polymers. Clay based adhesives are coloured and tend to have the lowest water content (40–50 per cent). They are used to stick heavier coverings. Clear vinyl adhesives are made from natural polymers such as wheat or corn starch, or from synthetic polymers.

Vinyl adhesive

When you apply the paste on some papers avoid over-pasting as the paste may soak through the paper or make the edges of the paper curl up. You also need to use vinyl adhesive when applying borders or overlapping vinyls.

ACTIVITY

Which types of paper would you stick with the following adhesives?

Adhesive	Types of paper
Cellulose adhesive	
Starch based paste	
Vinyl adhesive	

Wallpaper roll labels

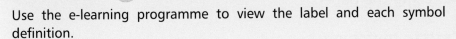

E-LEARNING

Use the e-learning programme to view the label and each symbol definition.

The wallpaper label will provide additional information about the properties of the paper to help you decide whether it is suitable for your project.

Batch number

The label on the rolls of paper will give you the batch number for the roll. Before buying, make sure that these match across all the rolls of paper for the job otherwise there may be variations in shading or colour.

Cleaning method

The label should give information on how to clean the wallpaper. It may be washable, extra-washable, spongeable or scrubbable. This will be important if you are papering high trafficked areas where the paper may get dirty. If there is no information on washability it does not necessarily mean it can be washed.

Fade resistance

The label may provide information on how resistant the paper is to fading. This is important if you plan to hang the paper in a sunny room. The colour may fade more quickly in sunnier conditions.

Pasting method

The label will tell you whether you will need to paste the back of the paper (the most common method) or the wall, or whether it is pre-pasted and you have to lay the paper in a trough of water to release the adhesive before offering up to the wall. Take care not to oversoak the paper. Make sure that all lengths are soaked for the same period of time otherwise you will have problems matching the paper.

Pattern matching

The label will tell you whether the pattern is random, a set pattern, or an offset or drop match pattern. If it is a drop match pattern, it will also tell you the distance the pattern is offset. This figure will affect the amount of paper needed.

Removal method

The label may also tell you how easy it is to remove the paper at a later date. You may be able to pull it away, strip it with water and a scraper or it may peel off, sometimes leaving a backing paper.

Pattern Number: 14005   **Batch Number:** C00012   **Design:** Autumn Leaves

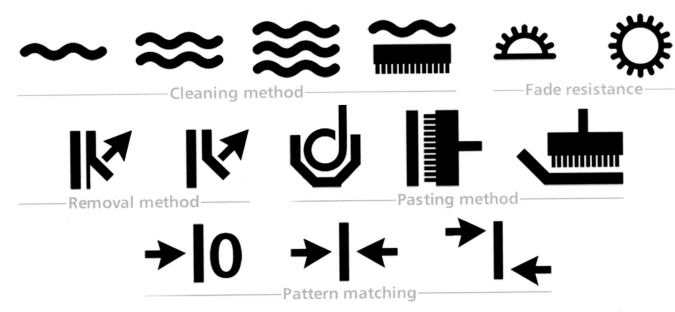

Check all rolls carry the same batch number. See over for tips on easy hanging.
Roll Size: 10m x 0.52m (11yds x 20.5 ins). Approx: 5.2m² (56ft²)

Wallpaper symbols

ACTIVITY

Visit a DIY store and identify the label on rolls of wallpaper to see information on the batch number and the different symbols.

Ordering wallcoverings

When wallpapering a room, it is important to order the correct amount to save on materials and costs. You will need to take into consideration the size and shape of the room as well as the type and style of paper.

You will need to allow for a small amount of overhang at the top and bottom of each length. If the wallcovering has a repeat pattern then you will need to order extra to ensure the pattern matches.

Surface area method

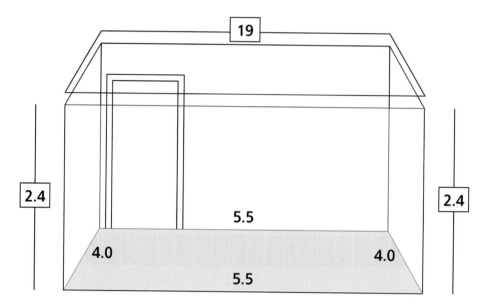

Example room measurements

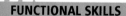

FUNCTIONAL SKILLS

In this example we are working in a room which is 5.5m long, 4m wide and 2.4m high. The room contains a standard door and window but we will include these in our calculations as it will contribute to the wastage amount. Wallpaper normally comes in lengths of 10.05m by 0.52m wide so therefore has a surface area of 5.226m squared.

1. First, calculate the perimeter of the room.
   5.5m + 5.5m + 4m + 4m = 19m

2. Multiply this by the height to get the surface area of the room.
   $19m \times 2.4m = 45.6m^2$

3. Divide the surface area of the room by the surface area of the roll of wallpaper.
   $45.6m^2 \div 5.226m^2 = 8.73$

Rounding up, we therefore require 9 rolls of wallpaper for this room.

ACTIVITY

You have to wallpaper a room with the following dimensions:

10m long

7m wide

3m high

The room contains a standard door and window but you should include these in the calculations as it will contribute to the wastage amount. Using the surface area method work out the following:

What is the perimeter of the room?

What is the surface area of the room?

How many rolls of wallpaper are required to paper the room?

Girthing method

The girthing method involves dividing the width of a roll of wallpaper into the perimeter of a room, and multiplying by the height of the walls. This can be done by physically stepping out with a roll of wallpaper, or mathematically. It is done to determine how many drops are needed, and to determine the start and end points.

Step out the wallpaper around the room

You can generally work out the amount of rolls required based on three to four drops per roll dependent on the height of the ceiling. Add 10 per cent for waste into your calculation.

Work out the drop pattern for your room

ACTIVITY

Using your answers from the previous activity, use the girthing method to work out how many rolls of wallpaper are needed. Which method do you prefer working with and why?

STORING AND DISPOSING OF TOOLS AND MATERIALS

This section looks at storing brushes and rollers, paint and wallpaper and disposal of materials.

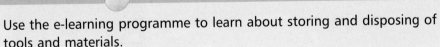

E-LEARNING

Use the e-learning programme to learn about storing and disposing of tools and materials.

Storing brushes and rollers

When storing your brushes and rollers make sure the stock on your brush does not become clogged in paint and avoid getting paint on the ferrule. Depending on the amount of time you are storing them, you can take different measures to make sure they stay in good condition.

Short breaks

For short breaks in painting, coat the brush or roller in paint and leave to stand for up to a few minutes.

Overnight storage

If you are not going to use a brush for a number of days, suspend the brush in water or put your roller sleeves in a plastic bag for short storage.

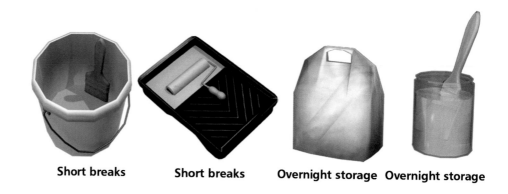

Short breaks   Short breaks   Overnight storage Overnight storage

Long-term storage

If you are not going to be using your brush or roller for a long time, wash them thoroughly and ensure they are completely dry.

Wash and dry your equipment thoroughly

Storing paint and wallpaper

Store paint and wallpaper in a dry place off the ground and away from direct sunlight and heat. Wipe the rim of paint tins clean before closing to ensure a good seal.

Make sure that wallpapers are stored horizontally to prevent damage to their edges and keep rolls with the same batch numbers together.

ACTIVITY

From the statements below fill in the missing gaps:

For short breaks in painting, coat the brush or roller in _____ and leave to stand for a few minutes.

If you are not going to use a brush for a number of days, suspend the

brush in _____ or put your roller sleeves in a _____ for short storage.

If you are not going to be using your brush or roller for a long time,

_____ and leave to dry completely.

Disposal of materials

SUSTAINABILITY

An estimated 366 million litres of paint are sold to the public and trade each year in the UK and 55 million litres are unused. They are either stored or thrown away. Stripped wallpaper is a major source of waste and it cannot be recycled with other paper recycling as it is likely to be contaminated. To reduce the amount of waste make sure you order only what you need for the project. If you do have any unused wallpaper or paint, it can be donated to community organizations. Do not throw paint or thinners down the drain. Dispose of stripped wallpaper and other materials through organizations licensed to dispose of waste. Remember that containers can be cleaned out and recycled.

CHECK YOUR KNOWLEDGE

1. **What is the purpose of each tool shown here? Match up the tools to their purpose.**

Task	Tool
Removing paint from beading	
Filling small holes	
Removing paint and wallpaper	
Abrading surfaces	
Removing wallpaper ONLY	

2. **What are the ingredients of paint?**

☐ a. Binder

☐ b. Pigment

☐ c. Solvent

☐ d. Polymers

3. **The symbols shown here are taken from wallpaper labels. What does each of them mean? Match up the symbols to the following meanings.**

Symbol	Meaning
	Scrubbable
	Paste the paper
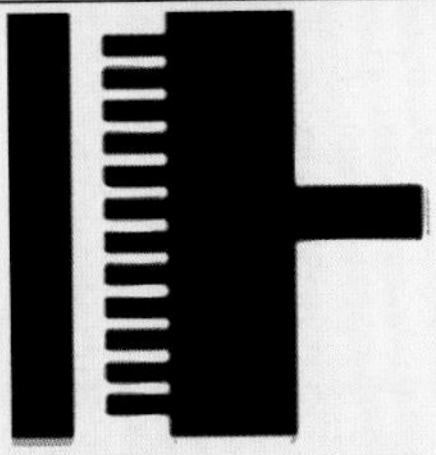	Random pattern
	Paste the wall
	Peelable

4. If you are not going to be using your brush or roller for a long time, wash them thoroughly and leave to dry completely. True or false?

☐ a. True

☐ b. False

5. Which adhesives tend to have the lowest water content (40–50 per cent)?

☐ a. Vinyl

☐ b. Clay based

Chapter 3

PREPARATION

LEARNING OBJECTIVES

By the end of this chapter you will be able to:

● Explain the importance of good preparation.

● List the steps needed to prepare the work area.

● List the factors that will influence the choice of preparation process.

● Explain the procedures for preparing different surfaces.

● Identify common defects in surfaces and how to correct them.

● List the steps for removing old wallpaper.

● Explain how to hang lining paper.

NOS REFERENCE

Prepare Surfaces for Painting and Decorating

Prepare New Surfaces for Paint Systems

Hang Wallcoverings (Standard Papers)

INTRODUCTION

Reasons for preparation

When painting and decorating, the preparation is as important as the finishing. Preparation involves making sure the surface is free of any defects that may show through, cleaning the surface of any grease or dirt and providing a good key for the covering to stick to.

Good preparation will ensure that the surface has a longer life because it will be well protected, and will make it look better for longer.

Clear the surface of dust and debris

HEALTH & SAFETY

Some surfaces or materials may be potentially harmful and contain **asbestos** or lead. For further information please refer to the **HSE** website.

WEBLINKS

Go to **www.hse.gov.uk** for the Health and Safety Executive website.

Asbestos A fibrous mineral commonly used in buildings as fireproofing material until the mid-1980s. Can be a health hazard and should not be disturbed. Seek specialist advice if found or suspected.

HSE Health and Safety Executive.

ACTIVITY

Using your existing health and safety knowledge and the Health and Safety Executive website, identify each of the symbols shown below and write down their meaning.

ACTIVITY

List some reasons why good preparation is important.

Preparing the working area

If you're re-decorating a room you will need to prepare your working area.

1. Begin by covering the floor leading to your working area.
2. Remove any objects that can be taken away and cover other objects.
3. Take down curtains and curtain rails.
4. Lift carpets, roll them up and place them in the middle of the room.
5. Cover the floor in the area you will be working in.
6. Remove **ironmongery** such as handles from doors and windows.
7. Check with your supervisor regarding any electrical or plumbing situations that may need to be considered.
8. If you are painting, use wet paint signs.

Ironmongery
Products that have been manufactured from metal.

Plan and prepare your working area

Remove or protect furniture and other surfaces

HEALTH & SAFETY

If you will be working at height make sure that platforms you are working on are properly secured. Let other people know that you will be working in that area, especially if you are going to be using electrical or pneumatic power tools such as sanders or steamers.

Assessment of surfaces

Before preparation you will need to check the surface to establish what needs to be done. Questions you will need to ask yourself include:

What is the surface? It could be wood, metal, plaster or **brickwork**; and different preparations will be required for each of them.

Second, what is the current condition of the surface? Preparation will be different for new and old surfaces. You will also need to check if there are any underlying problems such as damp, which should be resolved before starting work. What is the condition of any existing decoration? Old and flaking paint or wallpaper will need to be removed whilst a more stable surface could just be cleaned and covered.

Brickwork A solid wall built of bricks, laid to bond and in mortar. Used to be the most common load-bearing external wall construction. Mainly finished with fair faced bricks and pointed or rendered. Minimal maintenance required but as properties age partial or complete re-pointing or re-rendering respectively may become necessary.

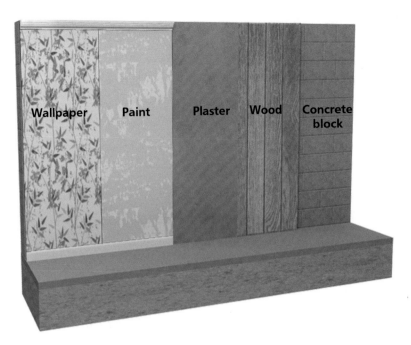

What surface will you be working on?

If you are working outdoors you will have to consider the weather conditions and the location. A surface that is likely to be subject to heavy rain will need different preparation to a surface subject to extreme sunlight. A range of temperatures could mean the surface will expand and contract.

Your preparation will need to make sure that the finish can move with the surface. Also, if you are working in colder or wet weather you may need to protect your work from the elements and it may take longer for paints to dry.

What conditions will you be working in?

ACTIVITY

What questions will you need to ask yourself when assessing the surfaces?

PREPARING WOOD SURFACES

This section looks at the different types of wood, preparing new and old wood, and treating defects in wood.

Types of wood

E-LEARNING

Use the e-learning programme to find out more about the types of wood.

Veneer Very thin sheets of finely grained woods used to improve the aesthetics and strength of sheet materials, e.g. blockboard.

Deciduous tree A tree that loses all of its leaves for part of the year.

Coniferous tree A type of evergreen tree that produces its fruit in the form of cones.

Hardwood

Hardwood is used for floors, doors and **veneers**. It is made from **deciduous trees** such as oak, beech, mahogany and walnut, and is typically finished in clear coats such as varnish or stains to enhance the appearance of the wood.

Softwood

Softwood is used for door and window frames and skirting boards. It is made from **coniferous trees** such as pine, cedar or spruce and would tend to be finished in opaque paints. It is usually finished in paint to cover knots.

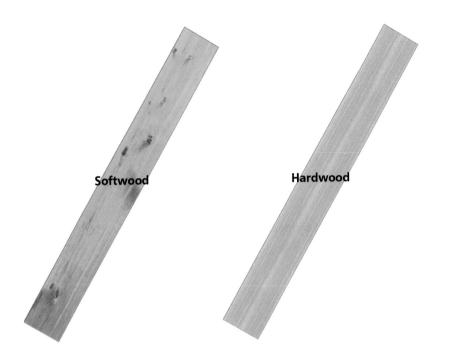

Softwood

Hardwood

Preparing new wood surfaces

The preparation for new softwood and hardwood surfaces is slightly different depending on the type of finish required.

E-LEARNING

Use the e-learning programme to see a demonstration on preparing softwood.

Softwood

1. Remove grease and stains and **abrade** with a medium to fine grain sandpaper. If there are any nails, push these below the surface and stop up the resulting holes with putty. You will also need to back fill any gaps and cracks with filler, and sand down when dry.

2. Apply two coats of knotting solution to any knots. This will protect against resin leaking out and staining the wood.

3. Finish by priming the wood with a recognized wood primer.

Abrade The wearing down of a particular material to make it suitable for the application of paint.

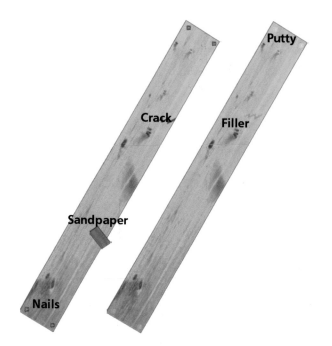

Putty

Crack

Filler

Sandpaper

Nails

Different types of wood require different methods of preparation

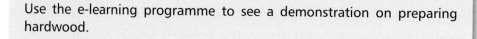

E-LEARNING

Use the e-learning programme to see a demonstration on preparing hardwood.

Hardwood

Being a premium material, hardwood should require little preparation. Your goal is to protect and enhance the natural wood finish.

1. Lightly abrade the surface going along the grain, never against. Going against the grain will scratch the surface. Abrading the surface will provide a key.

2. Dust off with a dust brush and wipe with a tack rag to remove fine surface dust. Some resinous timbers may require wiping down with white spirit to remove any excess resin.

3. If the wood contains defects or is damaged, these can be made good by filling any cracks or indentations with the correct colour filler or stopper for the wood that you are using.

Preparing old wood surfaces

Techniques for preparing previously painted wood surfaces will vary depending upon the condition of the paint.

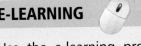

E-LEARNING

Use the e-learning programme to learn more about preparing old wood surfaces.

Sound paintwork

If the old paint is stable and not flaking it will not be necessary to remove; simply clean with sugar soap and sand down with a fine sandpaper to give a key for the paint. If there are any exposed edges to the paintwork, smooth these down with a fine sandpaper to give a flat finish. This is called feathering. If any timber is exposed apply knotting solution and primer as necessary.

Example of sound paintwork

Some preparation materials that can be used for paintwork

Flaking paintwork

If the paintwork is badly flaking, you will need to remove it. This can be done by using a hand or mechanical sander. In either case, start with a coarse grain sandpaper and work to a finer grade to ensure a smooth finish.

Preparation of flaking paintwork

Sanders can be used on large surfaces. A heat gun and shave hooks can be used for carved or shaped areas. Take care if applying heat on window frames to avoid cracking the glass. After you have removed the old paint, sand down and prime the surface.

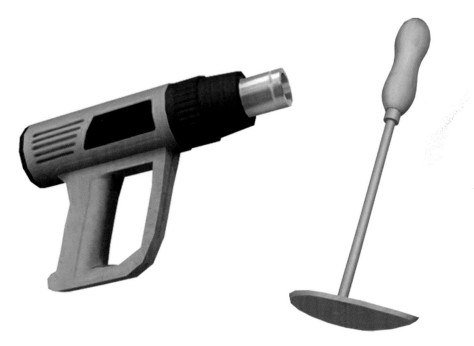

Different equipment can be used depending on how bad the surface is

Varnished wood

Previously varnished wood that will be painted or re-varnished can be cleaned and sanded down if it is reasonably sound. However, if you are planning to stain the wood, you will need to remove all of the old varnish with a varnish stripper and then clean the surface thoroughly so that the old varnish surface does not show through.

Example of a varnished surface

Solvent Paint
Remover

DANGER! ☠ POISON.
MAY BE FATAL OR CAUSE BLINDNESS IF SWALLOWED.
VAPOR HARMFUL. SKIN AND EYE IRRITANT. Read other
cautions and HEALTH HAZARD INFORMATION on back panel.
ONE GALLON 3.785 LITERS

A typical solvent based remover

HEALTH & SAFETY

Be extremely careful when using any solvents, they could be flammable, poisonous or extremely harmful.

ACTIVITY

Below are three pictures showing different wood conditions. Can you identify which is sound paintwork, flaking paintwork and varnished wood?

Treating defects in wood

Part of the preparation process will involve treating any defects in the wood. These can include treating knots and resin in new or old wood, removing decay from old wood and treating denatured timber.

E-LEARNING

Use the e-learning programme to see demonstrations on treating defects in wood.

Knots

Knots appear in timber where there was a joint with another branch. Many knots can be smoothed down and painted over. However loose knots will need to be removed and replaced with two pack filler.

Resin

Knots can also leak resin which will stain the surface of the wood. Apply two coats of knotting solution to the knot and make sure it is well brushed in beyond the edges of the knot. Leave for ten minutes before applying the second coat. Knots which leak excessive resin should be replaced with two pack filler.

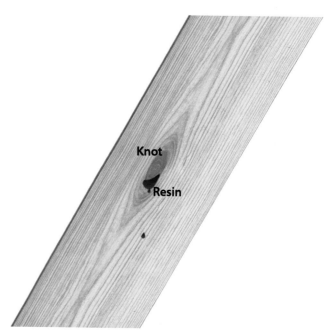

Example of a knot with seeping resin

Decayed wood

Decayed wood should be cut out completely and replaced with sound timber. Make sure that you cut out beyond the area of decay to avoid leaving any old wood which may later affect the rest of the surface. If the decay is extensive then the entire piece of timber will need to be removed. Treat the old and new wood with a **fungicide** before painting.

Fungicide A chemical used to kill or slow down fungal decay on timber.

De-natured timber

De-natured timber is sound timber that has been exposed to the elements, and is greyish in colour. Abrade the surface back to good timber with a medium sandpaper.

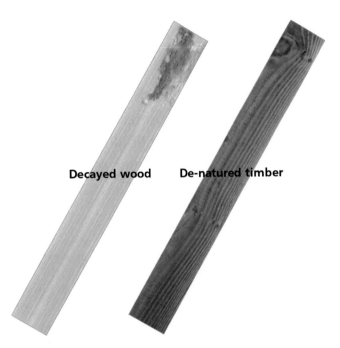

Decayed wood   **De-natured timber**

Example of decayed and de-natured timber

PREPARING PLASTERED AND RENDERED SURFACES

This section looks at the different types of plastered and **rendered** surfaces. It looks at preparing new and old plastered surfaces and preparing exterior rendered surfaces as well as treating defects in plastered and rendered surfaces.

Render A sand and cement backing coat for tiling, usually applied in at least two coats.

Types of plastered and rendered surfaces

When preparing plaster or rendered surfaces, the interior and exterior of a building will be different.

E-LEARNING

Use the e-learning programme to learn more about types of plastered and rendered surfaces.

Internal surfaces

Internal surfaces are generally covered with a plaster finish or **plasterboard**. Plasterboard is sometimes skimmed with a thin coat of plaster. This will take approximately two weeks to dry completely so preparation work should not start before then. Both surfaces are highly absorbent and will need priming before applying paint.

Plasterboard A type of board made of gypsum sandwiched between sheets of paper. It has a number of properties and can be made to different thicknesses and sizes for different areas and uses.

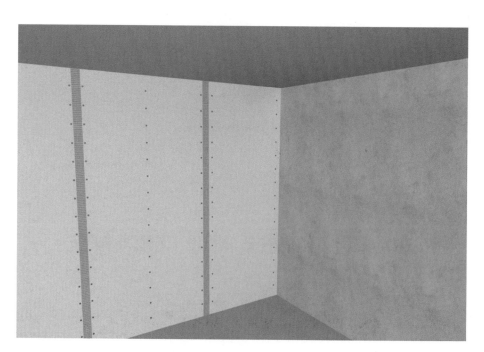

A typical internal surface of plaster or plasterboard

External surfaces

External surfaces are sometimes covered in a render which can be a mixture of **cement**, **sand** and lime and it must be completely dry before preparing for painting. This can take some time, typically six weeks or longer. If you attempt to paint a rendered surface too soon then you can seal in moisture which will lead to problems in the future.

Cement A grey or white powdery material made from chalk or limestone and clay. Cement is the most common binder in bricklaying mortar and works by hardening as a result of a chemical reaction when mixed with water. The most common type of cement is Ordinary Portland Cement (OPC).

Sand Fine aggregate that is one of the raw ingredients for mixing mortar.

External renders can suffer from moisture damage

Typical ingredients of a render mix

ACTIVITY

Below are two statements about types of plastered and rendered surfaces. Fill in the missing words:

Plasterboard is sometimes skimmed with a thin coat of _____.

External surfaces are sometimes covered in a render which can be a mixture of _____, _____ and _____

Preparing plaster surfaces

E-LEARNING

Use the e-learning programme to see a demonstration on preparing plaster surfaces.

Checks

Before applying paint or wallcoverings to a plaster surface, make sure that all moisture has evaporated and the surface is completely dry. Check for defects and ensure that the surface is smooth and flat. Scrape any plaster splashes and brush off any efflorescence (these are white crystals that rise to the surface as the plaster dries).

Plaster skim

For skimmed plaster, fill any defects with filler and lightly sand down the surface. New finished plaster should not need to be abraded other than to sand down any filler otherwise this could leave scratch marks in the polished surface. For a painted finish apply a primer of four parts emulsion to one part water.

Plasterboard

For plasterboard surfaces, make sure the joints have been taped, filled and sanded. Fill any screw holes, and use a proprietary sealer or primer before applying paint to the surface. If hanging to a plaster skim, the plaster would need to be sized with the appropriate diluted paste.

Wallpaper

Size with the appropriate diluted paste.

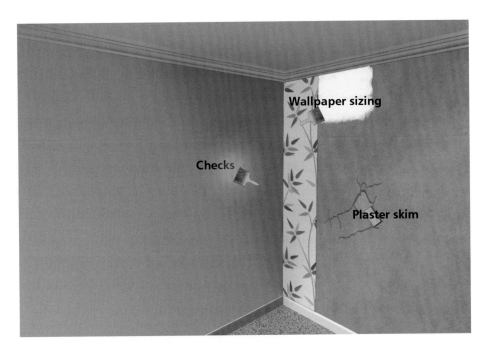

Carry out appropriate checks on plastered surfaces

Preparing exterior rendered surfaces

Preparation for a rendered surface will depend upon its condition.

E-LEARNING

Use the e-learning programme to see a demonstration on preparing exterior rendered surfaces.

New surfaces

A newly rendered surface will just need brushing down to remove any loose material.

Old surfaces

Older surfaces will need more treatment.

1. Apply a fungicidal wash to remove any mould or algae.

2. Wash with clean water and brush the wall down with a stiff brush to remove dead growth. Make sure that all the growth has gone otherwise it may show through after you have painted.

3. Brush the surface to remove any flaking paint, loose mortar and dust.

4. Fill any holes or cracks and apply a stabilizing masonry primer to an unsound surface making sure the surface is fully coated.

5. This will ensure a solid background ready for painting.

Mortar A mixture of sand, cement (sometimes with lime and/or additives) and water, used to bond stones and bricks. Can be mixed by hand or mechanically on- or off-site.

Check the condition of external render

Apply an appropriate solution to the render to help preparation

Treating defects on exterior surfaces

External render can be subject to a number of defects. Here are two of the most common.

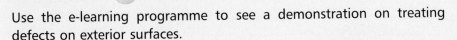

E-LEARNING

Use the e-learning programme to see a demonstration on treating defects on exterior surfaces.

Efflorescence

A common defect in rendered surfaces is efflorescence. These are white salts that can appear on the surface. The salt may have been in the brick or mortar used to build the wall and as the wall dries the water evaporates bringing the salts to the surface. Brush the efflorescence away and wait to see if it reappears.

Moisture penetration

Moisture penetration can be a particular problem for rendered surfaces. There will be damp patches and in some cases the

Cavity The gap between the internal and external walls of a building. Usually 50mm wide to increase the thermal insulation and weather resistance of the wall. The cavity must be kept clear and not bridged (except for wall ties and insulation). A damp proof course (DPC) must be provided around the perimeter of openings in cavity walls otherwise dampness can occur internally.

Rendering The application of render to external wall surfaces for appearance or to make the wall waterproof. Cracks may appear and should be repaired as progressively they will weather and lose key allowing water to get behind render. This causes saturation of the wall which can result in fungal decay of structural timbers internally.

render may fall away. This is usually as the result of poor protection against damp such as the lack of flashing and damp proofing. Other sources of damp could include water leaks from broken pipes or penetrating damp because of a blocked **cavity**. These will need to be remedied and the old render removed to allow the background to dry out before **rendering**.

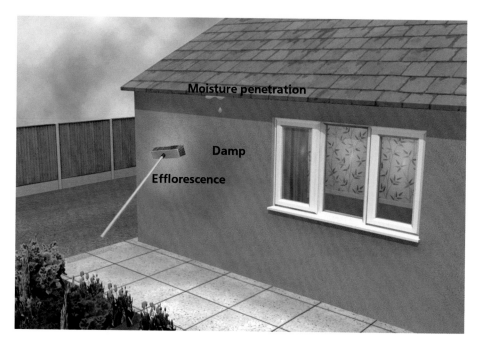

Example of moisture penetration, damp, and efflorescence

ACTIVITY

What is efflorescence? Write a brief description in your own words.

What is moisture penetration? Write a brief description in your own words.

PREPARING METAL SURFACES

This section looks at the different types of metal surfaces, preparing metal surfaces and treating defects on metal surfaces.

Types of metal surfaces

There are two types of metal: ferrous and non-ferrous.

Ferrous metals

Ferrous metals are prone to **corrosion** or rust which needs to be treated before finishing. New ferrous metals can suffer from mill scale. This is a thin layer of metal oxides which cover the metal when it leaves the rolling mill. With weathering and handling it can fall away taking any finishes covering it. New metal surfaces need to be prepared as thoroughly as older surfaces.

Non-ferrous metals

Non-ferrous metals do not have the strength to be used for structural purposes but tend to be used for coatings.

> **Corrosion** The damage of a material by a substance such as rain or water.

Metals can be ferrous and non-ferrous

Preparing metal surfaces

New metal surfaces may be coated with a thin film of oil to prevent corrosion. This will need to be removed with a solvent to make sure the paint can stick.

For all types of ferrous metals:

1. Remove rust and mill scale from the surface with a wire brush, emery cloth or a mechanical abrasion.

2. Wipe any dust or grease away.

3. As soon as possible apply a rust inhibiting primer to prevent corrosion re-occurring.

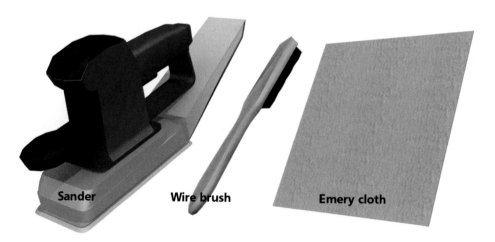

Tools and equipment that can be used to clean metal

ACTIVITY

For each of the metals below list whether it is ferrous or non-ferrous.

Metal	Type of metal
Copper	
Iron	
Steel	
Zinc	
Tin	
Aluminium	

Treating defects on metal surfaces

Metal can suffer from a number of defects. Here are two common defects.

E-LEARNING

Use the e-learning programme to see a demonstration on treating defects on metal surfaces.

Rust

Rusting is when iron in the metal reacts with oxygen in the presence of water. Other contributing factors to rusting include air moisture, air humidity and salts.

HEALTH & SAFETY

Severe corrosion will need to be removed with a chipping hammer or grinder. If this is the case then always remember your PPE.

A wire brush can be used for surface rust. Use a rust inhibiting primer immediately after removing rust to prevent re-occurrence.

To avoid rust appearing underneath paint do not paint metal surfaces at low temperatures, (below 4° Celsius) or high humidity (above 80 per cent), otherwise moisture will be trapped beneath the paint and the rust can come back.

Rusting metal and how it can be treated

ACTIVITY

What PPE do you think should be worn when removing rust with a chipping hammer or grinder?

Mill scale

Mill scale is formed in the manufacturing process and is a thin flaking film that forms on the surface of the metal. Remove the mill scale by using a wire brush and prime immediately. Failure to do this would lead to rusting.

Mill scale and how it can be treated

WALLPAPER PREPARATION

This section looks at removing old wallpaper, cross lining paper and hanging cross lining paper.

Removing old wallcoverings

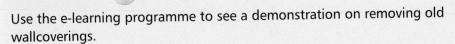

E-LEARNING

Use the e-learning programme to see a demonstration on removing old wallcoverings.

When removing old wallcoverings you will need to think about the condition and type of surface beneath the covering, the type and condition of the covering itself and how easy it is to remove the old covering.

1. Before attempting to remove all the paper it is a good idea to test a small section to see how easy it will come away.
2. Peel off any covering and soak a small area of the remaining paper.
3. Attempt to remove with a scraper or broad knife.
4. You may need to repeat the soaking process.
5. Large areas of wallpaper can be removed with a steamer and a scraper.

HEALTH & SAFETY

Take care when using a steamer and follow the manufacturer's instructions.

SUSTAINABILITY

After removal, consider the safe and sustainable disposal of the old covering.

Remove old wallpaper using the correct method

Hanging cross lining paper

If you are going to paper over the lining paper, hang horizontally to ensure good adhesion.

1. Measure down from the ceiling the width of a roll and strike a horizontal line at this point.

2. Set out your paper so you do not finish with thin strips at the bottom of the wall.

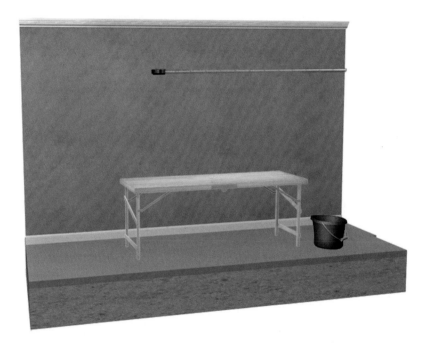

Measure the area to be covered

3. Measure the length of the wall, adding an extra 100mm.

4. Cut the paper to the length of the wall plus the extra 100mm, and lay it face down on the paste table.

5. Paste all of the paper.

Paste the lining paper correctly

6. Pick up the top edge of the paper and fold the first 300mm over.

7. Then pick up this fold and fold over a second time.

8. Continue until the paper is folded into a concertina.

9. You may need to lay it on another roll of paper to make it easier to lift.

Fold the paper into a concertina

10. Lift up the folded paper and apply to wall, holding the unfolded end in one hand and the concertina section in the other.

11. Push the end of the paper into the top corner, lining up the bottom edge with your guide line. Brush out the paper, unfolding as you go along, making sure there are no air bubbles. Continue hanging the next lengths below.

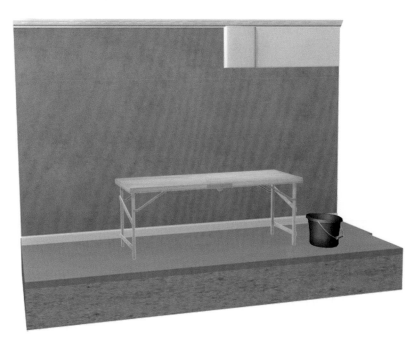

Position the paper on the surface

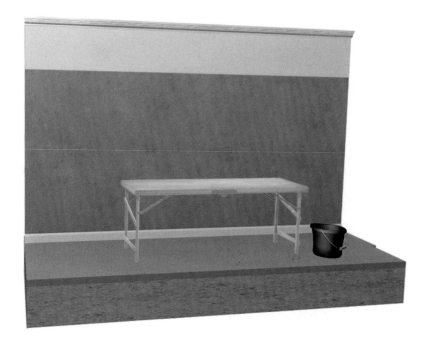

Make sure the paper is aligned

12. You may need to cut the last length along its width to make it fit.

13. Brush out the paper making sure there are no air bubbles.

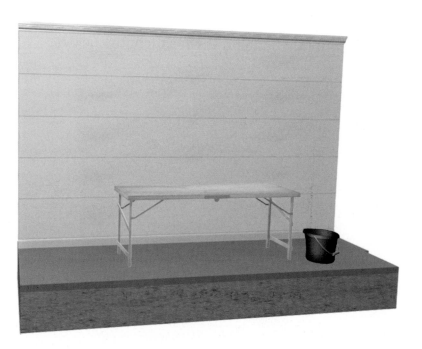

Continue working down the wall

ACTIVITY

Here is a list of instructions on hanging cross lining paper. Two of the steps are missing. Identify what these are, and then write them in the appropriate place in the list.

• Measure down from the ceiling the width of a roll and strike a horizontal line at this point.

• Set out your paper so you do not finish with thin strips at the bottom of the wall.

• Cut the paper to the length of the wall plus the extra 100mm, and lay it face down on the paste table.

• Paste all of the paper.

• Then pick up this fold and fold over a second time.

• Continue until the paper is folded into a concertina.

• You may need to lay it on another roll of paper to make it easier to lift.

• Lift up the folded paper and apply to wall, holding the unfolded end in one hand and the concertina section in the other.

• Push the end of the paper into the top corner, lining up the bottom edge with your guide line. Brush out the paper, unfolding as you go along, making sure there are no air bubbles. Continue hanging the next lengths below.

• You may need to cut the last length along its width to make it fit.

• Brush out the paper making sure there are no air bubbles.

CHECK YOUR KNOWLEDGE

1. **How long should you wait before painting a plaster skimmed surface?**

   ☐ a. 1 day

   ☐ b. 1 week

   ☐ c. 2 weeks

   ☐ d. 6 weeks

   ☐ e. 2 months

2. **What should the humidity level not be above when you are painting a metal surface?**

   ☐ a. 20 per cent

   ☐ b. 40 per cent

   ☐ c. 50 per cent

   ☐ d. 80 per cent

3. **Hardwood is used for floors, doors and veneers. Is this:**

   ☐ a. True

   ☐ b. False

4. **Softwood is made from oak trees. Is this:**

   ☐ a. True

   ☐ b. False

5. **If the paintwork is badly flaking, should you remove it?**

   ☐ a. Yes

   ☐ b. No

Chapter 4

PAINTING

LEARNING OBJECTIVES

By the end of this chapter you will be able to:

- Explain the basic principles of the colour theory.

- Understand the sequence of applying paint to a room.

- Understand the techniques for applying paint to different types of surfaces.

NOS REFERENCE

Apply Paint Systems by Brush and Roller

COLOUR THEORY

This section looks at how we see colours, primary and secondary colours, choosing colours and colour systems.

E-LEARNING

Use the e-learning programme to see a demonstration on how we see colours.

How we see colours

The light we see is made up of different wavelengths. When all the wavelengths are combined the light appears white. When the light is split through a **prism** we can see the different wavelengths shown as different colours. When the light hits an object, certain wavelengths are absorbed but other are reflected. It is the light that is reflected back that enables us to see the colour of the object.

Prism A clear object which separates white light into a spectrum of different colours.

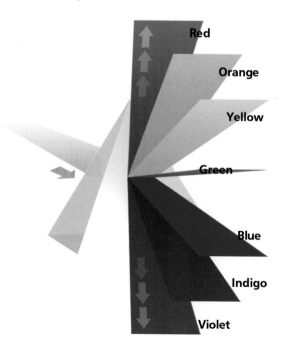

The colours that make up visible light

Primary and secondary colours

Primary colours are sets of colours that can be mixed to form a range of other colours. RYB (red, yellow, blue) is used when mixing pigments and paints. When mixed together they will produce a black, although the resulting colour is likely to be a grey because of impurities within the pigment. These are known as subtractive mixtures. The RYB system is the oldest colour system and is the one used in painting and decorating.

Secondary colours are the colours made by mixing two of the primary colours. For example, red and yellow make orange, red and blue make purple and blue and yellow make green.

**Primary colours in an RYB system
(Red, Yellow and Blue)**

**Secondary colours in an RYB system
(Orange, Purple and Green)**

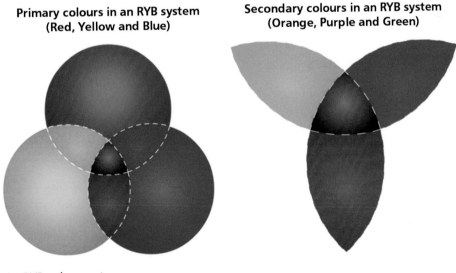

An RYB colour system

ACTIVITY

In the table shown, write down whether each of the colours is primary or secondary.

Colour	Type of colour
Purple	
Red	
Green	
Orange	
Yellow	
Blue	

Choosing colours

E-LEARNING

Use the e-learning programme to see a demonstration on choosing colours.

This common set of colours provides a good basis for deciding on a choice of colours and colour schemes. Colours close to each other in the set are harmonious, whilst colours further apart can be complementary or contrasting to each other. This can be dramatic and needs to be handled carefully; colours in small contrasts can work by accenting colour schemes.

Darken or lighten colours by adding black or white. This creates shades and tints. A dark colour would absorb more light so it would make a room look darker than a light colour. A scheme can be based upon shades of a single colour. Red, orange and yellow are warm colours whilst the blues and greens are cold colours.

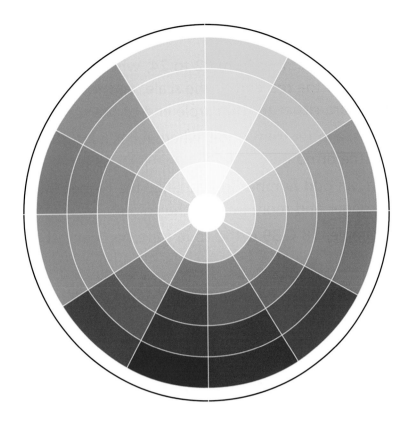

A simple colour wheel

Colour codes and finishes

Paint manufacturers will give their paints distinctive names to differentiate them from similar products on the market, for example, Ocean Blue, Fathom Blue or Azure Blue. These names could in fact be describing the same shade of blue paint.

NOTE ON UK STANDARDS

British Standard BS4800, Paint Colours for Building Purposes, assigns a code for each paint colour used in the building trade so that it can be identified even if it has a different name from a different company. This number is the same across manufacturers.

The British Standard code is made up of three parts:

- Hue, an even number from 02 to 24, where lower numbers are closer to the red end of the scale, and the higher numbers are closer to the purple end of the scale.
- Greyness, a letter from A to E where A has a lot of grey whilst E has little or no grey.
- Weight, an odd number from 01–55, the higher the number the stronger and more intense the colour.
- For example, 18 C 39 is the code for a particular shade of blue.

Symbols are sometimes used to tell you the finish of the paint.

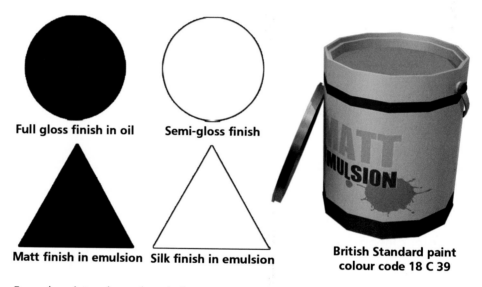

Full gloss finish in oil   Semi-gloss finish

Matt finish in emulsion   Silk finish in emulsion

British Standard paint colour code 18 C 39

Example paint codes and symbols

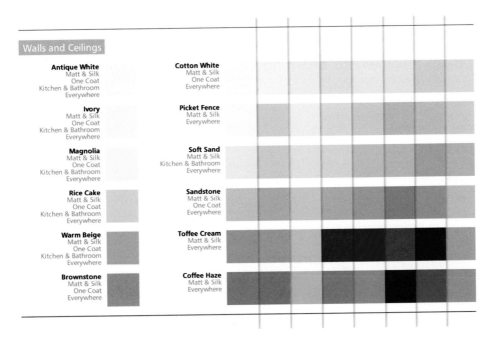

Example paint colour chart

APPLYING PAINT

This section looks at the order for painting a room, techniques for applying paint, painting walls and ceilings, painting wood-work and drying times.

Order for painting a room

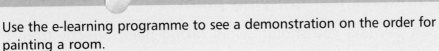

E-LEARNING

Use the e-learning programme to see a demonstration on the order for painting a room.

There are various sequences for painting a room but most of them involve starting with the ceiling, painting the **cornices** (if they need to be done separately), painting the walls (usually beginning around the windows) and finally painting the windows, radiators and doors. The general order is starting at the top (the ceiling) and working your way to the exit (the door). This order has two advantages. By starting at the top

> **Cornice** A decorative moulding at the junction between the walls and ceiling of a room.

and working your way down paint from the ceiling will only drip onto undecorated areas. By working your way towards the exit you are less likely to brush against wet paint.

ACTIVITY

Identify the sequence for painting a room by writing the step number on the image below.

Techniques for applying paint

When painting you should avoid taking paint directly from the tin as this could lead to contamination. A thick film of coat on the brush will make it easier to apply and the edge of the paint will stay wet longer so that you have more time to work it in. This is called a longer wet edge time. There will also be less brush marks and you will apply a fuller and more even and durable coat. Insufficient paint will result in an uneven finish with gaps, wrinkles, sags and runs.

Pour paint into a paint kettle

E-LEARNING

Use the e-learning programme to see a demonstration on applying paint.

Applying paint to the brush

Pour the paint to be used into a **paint kettle**. Make sure the brush has sufficient paint to apply a full coat to the surface. It should be about a third of the bristle length.

Paint kettle When painting, pour the paint into one of these to stop contamination of the manufacturer's paint tin.

Coat the brush with the paint

Applying paint to the roller

If using a roller, make sure you do not overload it. Roll it back-wards and forwards in the tray to ensure an even spread.

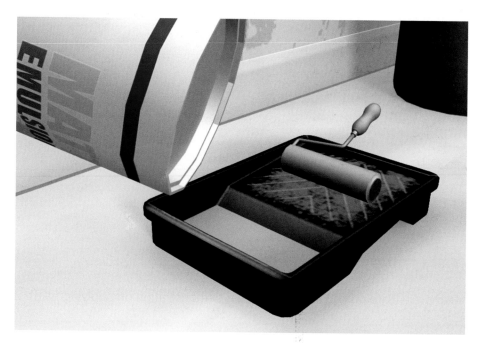

Coat the roller with the paint

Painting walls and ceilings

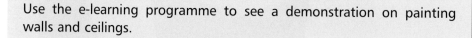

E-LEARNING

Use the e-learning programme to see a demonstration on painting walls and ceilings.

When decorating, you should always paint the ceiling before the walls. For both surfaces, your first step is to cut in. This is painting a two to three inch strip around the corners and around any fittings or fixtures. You should do this on one wall at a time.

1. Split the surface into manageable areas and work in stages. When painting a ceiling, start in the corner furthest away from the door. With a wall, always paint top to bottom.

2. If using a brush to paint then it must have a good coating of paint. You can apply the paint in all directions making sure that you apply a firm and even coating whilst checking the paint doesn't run.

3. If using a roller, the same principles apply, however you can use the M and W techniques to roll the paint on in the shape of these letters to get good wall coverage. Use a steady motion to reduce splatter marks.

The number of coats applied will make a difference. On some occasions it may be more beneficial to apply two thin coats rather than one thick one.

Split your areas of painting into manageable sections

Painting windows and doors

Woodwork will need to be painted differently depending on the type of window or door you are painting.

E-LEARNING

Use the e-learning programme to find out more about painting windows and doors.

Flush doors

For a flush door with a plain surface, paint in stages of around 300mm by 300mm. Don't forget to paint the edges of the door as well. If you are painting a door that opens away from you, paint the hinge edge as well as the face. If you are painting a door that opens towards you, paint the latch edge.

Painting a flush door in small sections

Muntin Vertical intermediate timbers between the panels of a door.

Stile Upright framing of a door into which the ends of the horizontal rails are fixed.

Panelled doors

If you are painting a panelled door, start with the edges of the door, followed by the panels and surrounding mouldings, and then the **muntins**. Now move on to the top, middle and bottom rails, and finish by painting the left and right **stiles**.

ACTIVITY

In what order do you think this panelled door should be painted? Number the steps shown.

Windows

The process for painting windows will vary depending upon the type. In general, however, work from top to bottom and from side to side. Paint the glazing bars, followed by the top and bottom rail of the opener, then the stiles and the muntin. Finish with the header and the **cill**.

Cill The sloping piece below a window for rainwater to run off.

ACTIVITY

In what order do you think this window should be painted? Number the steps shown.

Drying times

Paint dries as the solvent within it evaporates leaving the resin and pigment to harden. The drying time will vary depending upon the type of paint. An emulsion may be **touch dry** in one to two hours, whereas gloss paint may take over four hours. Being touch dry is not the same as being re-coatable and it may take longer for the paint to be ready for another coat. Typical drying times will usually appear on the paint can. There are a number of factors that could impact upon the time it takes for the paint to dry. These can include extremes in temperature or humidity, or poor preparation of the surface or application of the paint.

Touch dry The stage during the drying of paint where it can be touched lightly without lifting any of the paint from the surface.

CHECK YOUR KNOWLEDGE

1. **The primary colour system used in painting and decorating is made up of which three colours?**

   ☐ a. Red

   ☐ b. Yellow

   ☐ c. Orange

   ☐ d. Green

   ☐ e. Blue

   ☐ f. Indigo

   ☐ g. Violet

   ☐ h. Black

2. **Label the RYB colour system below using the colours listed.**

   a. Red

   b. Orange

   c. Blue

   d. Purple

   e. Black

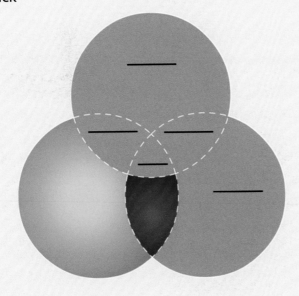

3. Secondary colours are the colours made by mixing two of the primary colours.

☐ a. True

☐ b. False

4. When painting which should you paint first?

☐ a. Walls

☐ b. Ceiling

Chapter 5

HANGING WALLCOVERINGS

LEARNING OBJECTIVES

By the end of this chapter you will be able to:

- Explain the impact of the starting point.

- Identify appropriate starting points in typical rooms.

- List the steps required to prepare the surface.

- Understand the technique for applying paper to walls.

- Understand the technique for applying paper to ceilings.

INTRODUCTION

Checklist for hanging paper

Before you start, check you have all the tools, equipment and materials you need for the project. Make sure that the rolls of paper all have the same batch number, check the type of pattern and that the adhesive is compatible with the wallpaper.

ACTIVITY

List all the tools, equipment and materials you think you will need when hanging wallpaper.

Preparing the surface

E-LEARNING

Use the e-learning programme to see a demonstration on preparing the surface.

Before papering make sure all old wallpaper and adhesive residue has been removed as the new covering is unlikely to hold if any remains. If the surface was previously painted, make sure it is in a sound condition and there are no signs of flaking paint. Water soluble paints will need to have been removed, and sealed with the appropriate primer. Oil-based gloss paints need to be abraded to provide a key. Plaster surfaces will need to be sized. This will help the adhesive dry evenly, help its holding power, and aid the slip of paper. Apply a dilute solution of the wallpaper adhesive to size the walls.

Prepare your background surface correctly

THE STARTING POINT

This section looks at the starting point for un-patterned and patterned papers, and hanging paper around staircases.

It is important to choose the starting and finishing point for hanging wallcoverings to make sure that the pattern matches up in the most visible point and any mismatches are inconspicuous.

E-LEARNING

Use the e-learning programme to find out more about the starting point for un-patterned and patterned papers.

Starting point: un-patterned paper

On most occasions, the starting point for un-patterned paper would be next to the source of natural light.

1. Begin by getting a straight line to hang the paper.
2. At the top of the wall measure out a width of the roll of paper, hang a plumb line from the mark, and draw a line down.
3. Work away from the light source so no shadows are cast over the paper joints.

Plumb line Length of string with weight attached, for checking vertical lines.

Ensure you mark out a plumb starting point

Work away from the light source

When papering into a corner, measure out the width between the previously hung length of paper and the corner of the wall, adding an extra 5 to 10mm to cover the turn. Hang a plumb line and draw a line down, placing the off-cut of paper tight into the corner of the wall.

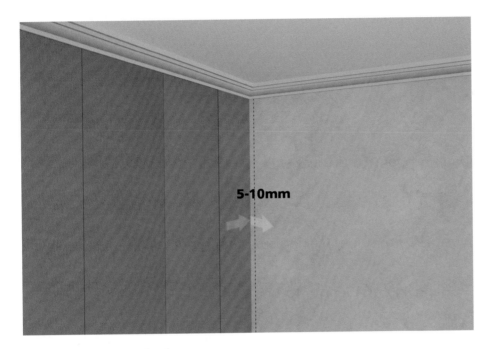

Add an extra 5-10mm for the turn

Place paper tight to the corner

Starting point: patterned paper

If you are hanging patterned paper, you should start either in the middle of your focal wall or on a prominent feature such as a chimney breast.

E-LEARNING

Use the e-learning programme to see a demonstration on hanging patterned paper.

Focal wall

Hanging paper to a focal wall:

1. Measure out the centre of the wall and draw a line down.

2. Calculate how many widths of paper fit the wall from both sides of this line, making sure that the final lengths are not too narrow.

3. Hang the first length to one side of the centre line, working away from the source of natural light.

4. If the lengths at the end of the wall are too narrow, centre the first length of paper and continue working away from the source of natural light.

Mark centre line of focal wall

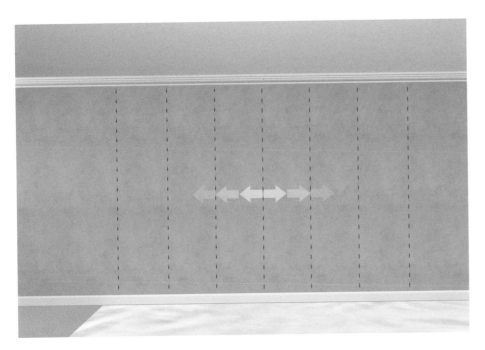

Plan the amount of sheets of paper needed

Begin from the side of the marked starting point

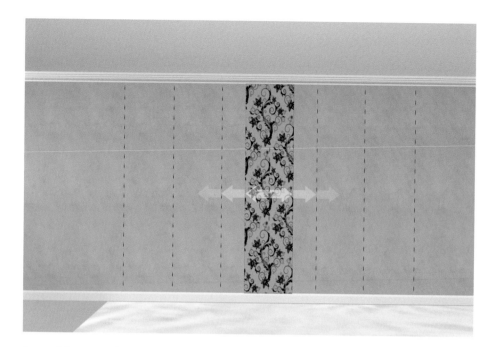

Re-position over the starting point if required

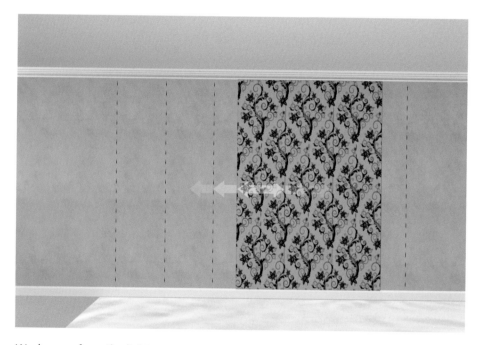

Work away from the light source

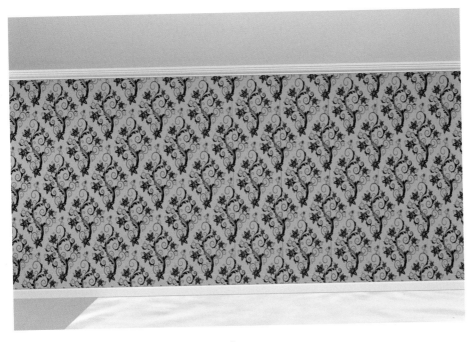

Continue along the focal wall until complete

Prominent feature

Hanging paper to a prominent feature, such as a chimney breast:

1. Measure out the centre of the wall and draw a line down.
2. Calculate how many widths of paper fit the wall from both sides of this line, making sure that the final lengths are not too narrow.
3. Hang the first length to one side of the centre line, working away from the source of natural light.
4. If the ends of the wall are too narrow, centre the first length of paper and continue working away from the source of natural light.
5. When turning an external corner, measure the width between the edge of the previously hung length of paper and the corner of the wall, and add an extra 25mm.
6. Once the length is hung, place the off-cut length of paper tight to the corner overlapping the extra 25mm of the previous length.

Mark centre line of feature

Begin from the side of the marked starting point

Work away from the light source

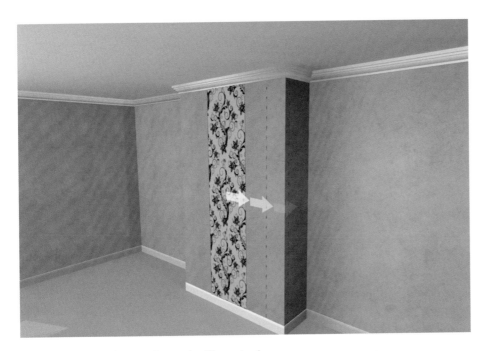

Re-position over the starting point if required

Check position of papers in regards to corners and patterns

Continue along the feature and remaining wall until complete

Hanging paper around staircases

E-LEARNING

Use the e-learning programme to see a demonstration of hanging paper around staircases.

When hanging paper around staircases, plumb the longest length first. Then paper the stairwell. Move upstairs to do the landing and then finish downstairs.

> Plumb The vertical level of a surface or structure.

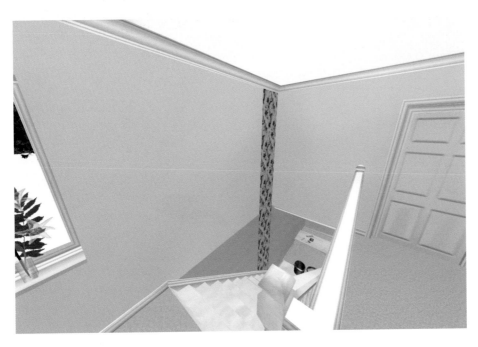

Start at the point with the longest drop

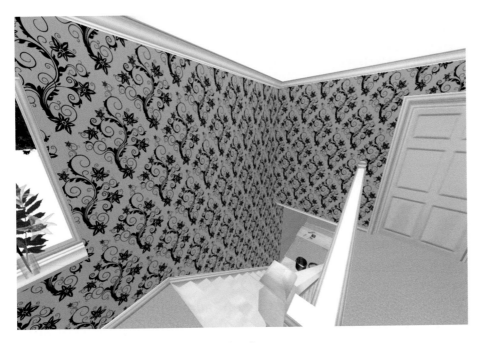

Wallpaper the stairway followed by the landing

Finish by doing the downstairs area

CUTTING AND PASTING THE PAPER

This section looks at cutting the paper, pasting the paper and using ready pasted paper.

Cutting paper

E-LEARNING

Use the e-learning programme to see a demonstration of cutting paper.

If the pattern is a straight match, cut from one roll at a time. If it is a drop match pattern then you should cut from two rolls to match up the pattern, this also avoids excess waste.

1. Measure and cut the first length adding on approximately 80mm for waste and ensure a full pattern motif is kept at the top of the paper.

2. Once the first length has been checked for accuracy, subsequent lengths can now be matched on the paste table

and cut from the two rolls. With experience and confidence you will be able to cut more lengths before pasting but this can be costly if mistakes are made.

Specialist rolls of paper may have a protective strip called a selvedge along their edges. This should be trimmed before pasting.

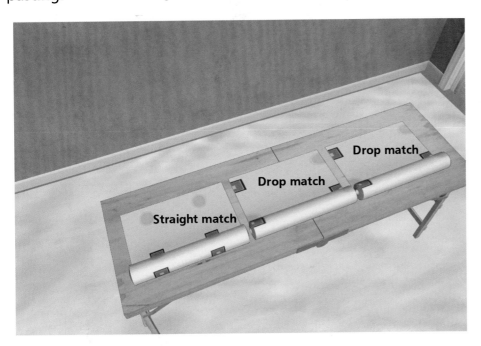

Use the correct amount of rolls depending on the pattern

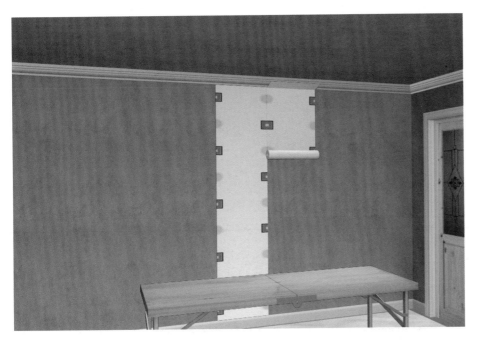

Leave enough material so you can match the pattern before trimming later

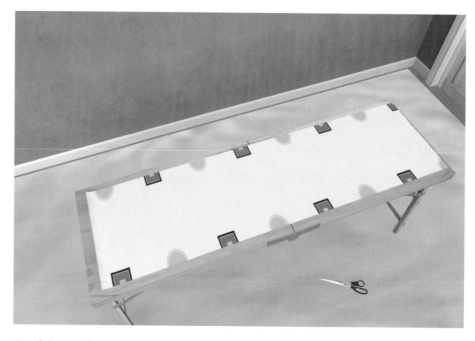

Carefully cut the paper to the required length

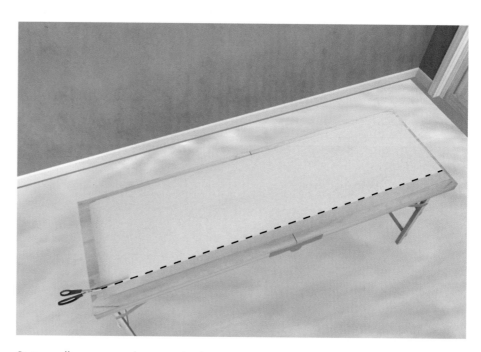

Some wallpapers may have a selvedge

ACTIVITY

Fill in the missing words from the following text about cutting paper.

Measure and cut the first length adding on approximately _____ for waste and ensure a full pattern motif is kept at the top of the paper.

Specialist rolls of paper may have a protective strip called a _____ along their edges.

Pasting paper

E-LEARNING

Use the e-learning programme to see a demonstration of pasting paper.

Before papering:

1. Cover the floor with a **dust sheet** and set up the paste table in the middle of the room.

2. Place the paste bucket on the floor next to the table. Don't put the bucket on the table as you might spill paste. It's a good idea to stretch a length of string across the top of the paste bucket to remove excess paste from the bush and as a rest for the brush.

3. Place a container such as a cardboard box or an empty bucket underneath the table to collect waste paper.

4. Include an additional bucket of clean warm water and a sponge ready for cleaning paste from any adjacent walls.

5. Make sure you use a paste that is compatible with the paper.

6. Place the paper on the pasting table face side down, aligning the edge of the paper with the edge of the pasting table.

7. Brush the paste from the centre to the edges, do one half first then move the paper to the other edge of the table and finish pasting.

8. Fold the edges of the paper into the middle ready for hanging on to the wall.

> **Dust sheet** A piece of material which protects household items from any spills, drips and dust during decorating.

Make sure you have all your materials and equipment prepared

Paste from centre to edges

Ready pasted paper

E-LEARNING

Use the e-learning programme to see a demonstration of using ready pasted paper.

Some types of wallpapers come with a dried paste backing. The paper needs to be soaked to activate the paste. This can be done by placing rolled up lengths of the wallpaper in a trough of cold water placed next to the wall to be covered. Then, draw the top edge of the paper out of the trough and position it on the wall. Smooth and trim the paper. The process can be messy so place plenty of covering around the work area and clean up any adhesive as you go along.

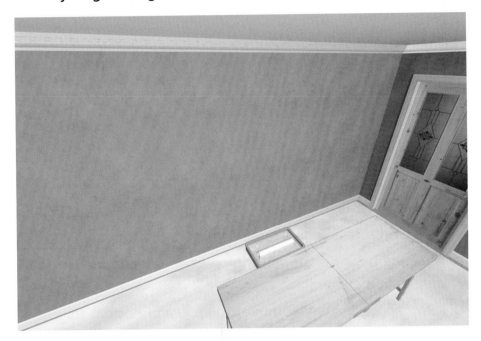

Soak the paper for the suggested amount of time

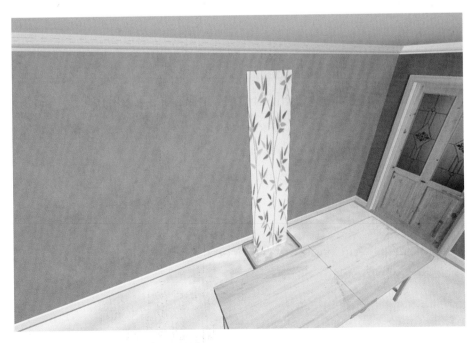

Position and smooth on to the wall

HANGING PAPER ON WALLS

This section looks at hanging the paper and cutting around objects.

Hanging the paper

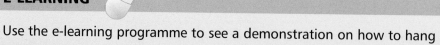

E-LEARNING

Use the e-learning programme to see a demonstration on how to hang paper.

When you have pasted and folded the paper, you are ready to starting hanging the paper.

1. Lift the folded paper carefully from the pasting table.
2. Start at the ceiling and carefully unfold the top half.
3. Place the paper at the starting point you determined in the preparation stage.
4. Leave approximately 40mm at the top and bottom for trimming.
5. When paper is in position, drop the bottom fold and smooth the paper down.
6. Smooth out any air bubbles with a damp sponge, papering brush or a wallpaper spatula.
7. Use a seam roller to smooth down the edge of the paper.
8. Press the paper into the top of the **skirting** board and mark with the back of the scissors.
9. Lift the paper away slightly and cut along the mark.
10. Push the paper back into place and wipe away any excess paste.
11. Make sure you wipe any adjacent surfaces with a sponge and clean warm water.

Skirting A moulding covering the joint formed by a wall and the floor.

Take care when lifting the paper

Position in pre-planned area

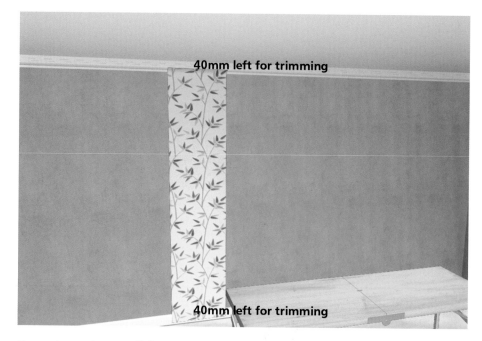

40mm left for trimming

40mm left for trimming

Remember to leave a slight excess of paper over the edges

Push paper into place and trim off the excess

Cutting around objects

You will need to trim the wallpaper around objects such as light fittings, switches and sockets, and door and window frames.

HEALTH & SAFETY

Make sure that the electricity has been switched off before papering around switches and light fittings. Check with the supervisor on who is responsible for carrying out all electrical work. Do not proceed if you are unsure about the current situation.

E-LEARNING

Use the e-learning programme to see a demonstration on cutting around objects.

Switches and sockets

1. Undo the retaining screws for the switch or socket and hang the paper lightly over the top.

2. Press gently over the object to find the corners and then cut the paper from the centre to each corner.

3. Gently ease the paper back and trim, leaving a small excess of paper to be tucked beneath the fitting.

4. Push the paper beneath the switch or socket and lightly tighten the retaining screws.

5. When the paper has dried tighten the screws fully.

Undo the retaining screws of the socket

Hang the paper over the socket

Find corners and cut back to the edge of the socket

Trim edges and fix socket back in place

Doors and windows

1. Hang paper lightly over the frame and mark the corners.
2. Cut back from the waste paper to the corners and smooth the paper onto the wall and against the edge of the frame.
3. Trim the paper from the edge of the frame.

Ensure the frame area is fully prepared

The process is the same for more complex edges such as fireplaces, although more care will be needed when trimming around the edges of the object.

Hang the paper and mark the frame edge

Cut the paper around the edge

Trim the edges for a neat finish

HANGING PAPER TO A CEILING

This section looks at preparation, cutting and pasting ceiling paper, hanging ceiling paper and cutting around ceiling roses.

Preparation

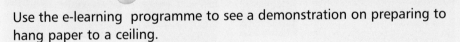

E-LEARNING

Use the e-learning programme to see a demonstration on preparing to hang paper to a ceiling.

The first part of the preparation process is to identify the starting point. This will depend upon the type of paper and the shape and size of the room.

If you are hanging non-patterned paper:

Measure one paper width away from the wall nearest a window and start hanging the paper from this line.

Non-patterned paper – find starting point

Non-patterned paper – hang paper from this point

If you are hanging patterned paper:

Find the centre line and plan out your sheets of paper so they are symmetrical and don't leave small cuts at the edge of the ceiling. This process is similar to marking out a wall.

Patterned paper – find the centre line of the ceiling

Patterned paper – match up paper pattern

Patterned paper – plan so the pattern is symmetrical

Patterned paper – don't leave small gaps at the edge of the ceiling

If the room is irregularly shaped:

Hang the longest length of paper and work away from it in both directions.

You should aim to work away from the source of natural light so it doesn't cast shadows over your joins.

Cutting and pasting ceiling paper

When preparing to hang ceiling paper, measure the width of the ceiling and add an extra 40mm. Cut the length of paper to this measurement and paste. Fold the paper into a concertina so that it will be easier to lift and apply to the ceiling.

Measure and cut your paper leaving a slight excess

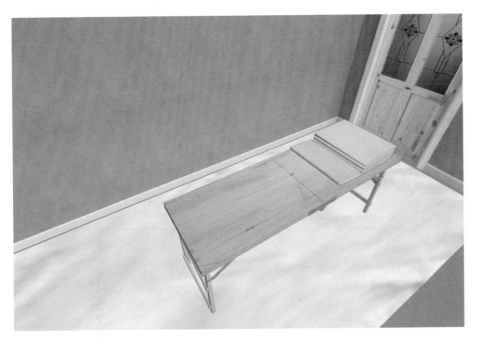

Paste and fold into a concertina ready for hanging

Hanging ceiling paper

E-LEARNING

Use the e-learning programme to see a demonstration on hanging paper to a ceiling.

1. Unfold the first concertina fold and push the paper up against the edge of the ceiling, allowing a little overlap down the wall. You may need to use some support to hold the paper in place. Smooth the paper against the ceiling, making sure there are no bubbles and the paper is tight against the wall.

2. Work backwards across the ceiling brushing the paper into place as it is unfolded.

3. When you have finished, mark on the paper where the ceiling and wall meet.

4. Lift back the paper and cut along the line.

5. Continue with the next length of paper, butting it against the first.

6. The final piece of paper will probably need to be cut length-ways in order to fit.

7. When you have hung the last but one length of ceiling paper, measure from its outside edge to the wall. Take this measurement and add another 50mm for overlap.

8. Cut the last length of paper to this width and hang it in the same way except this time you will need to trim the side as well as the ends.

HEALTH & SAFETY

Make sure you have a safe and adequate platform set up to accommodate the running length of the paper.

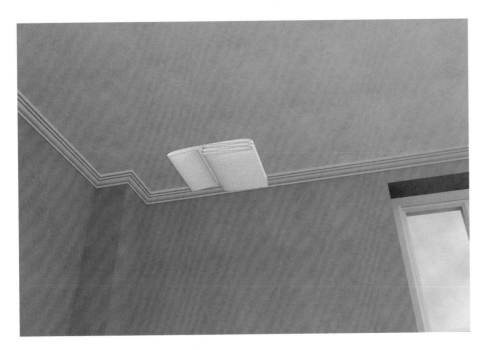

Begin unfolding the concertinaed paper

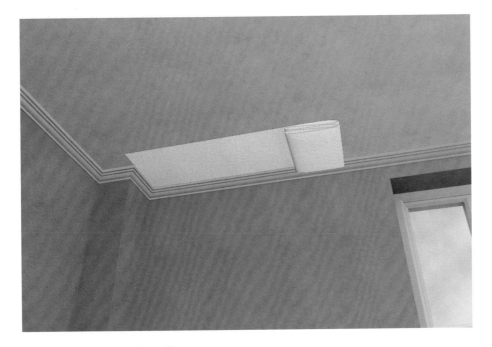

Smooth paper on to the ceiling

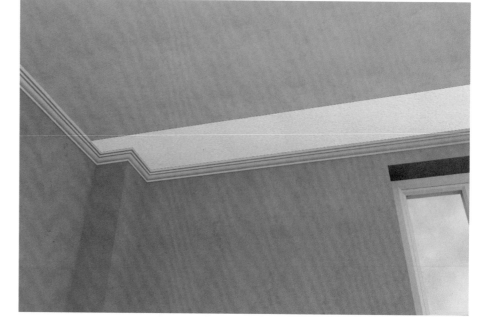

Work backwards across the ceiling

Mark on the paper where the ceiling and wall meet

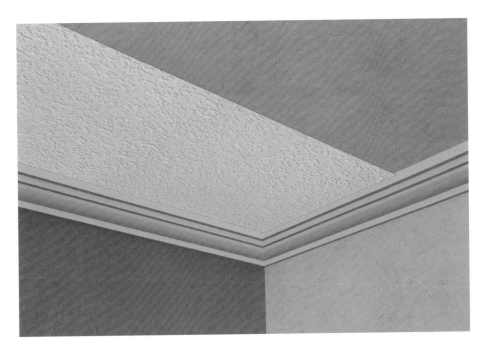

Trim excess for a neat finish

Ensure there are no gaps between the papers

End pieces may require some overlap for positioning

Once in place trim the end and side of the final piece

Cutting around objects

E-LEARNING

Use the e-learning programme to see a demonstration on cutting around objects.

HEALTH & SAFETY

When dealing with all electrical objects ensure that the electricity is switched off before papering. Check with your supervisor before doing any work around electrical items.

At some point you will need to paper around a ceiling light or ceiling rose. For a ceiling light, the simplest process is to remove the light fitting, leaving the cables, and hang the paper over the hole for the light fitting. Finish by trimming along the hole leaving a small amount of overlap but ensuring that the paper has no way of touching or sticking to the wires. When the paper and paste has dried and is firmly in place, refit the light fitting.

For large ceiling roses you may wish to arrange the paper so that the first length overlaps half the rose. Mark around the rose on the paper and cut triangles back from the edge of the paper to the marks. Push the paper up against the ceiling and the rose and trim the paper back.

Remove the light fitting

Hang the paper over the socket, mark the outline and cut back triangles

Trim the excess around the socket leaving a neat finish

Plan the positioning of your paper over the ceiling rose

Cut the paper from the rose centre to the edge and fold back in triangles

Trim the edges around the rose

CHECK YOUR KNOWLEDGE

1. **Which of the following starting points could be used for hanging wallpaper?**

   ☐ a. The centre of the focal point of the room

   ☐ b. The corner of the room

   ☐ c. Next to a natural source of light

2. **What type of pattern is the wallpaper shown here?**

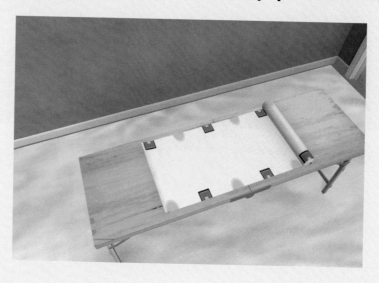

☐ a. Drop match

☐ b. Straight match

☐ c. Random

☐ d. Plain

3. When hanging paper around a staircase which length do you plumb first?

☐ a. Shortest

☐ b. Longest

4. If the paper is a drop match pattern how many rolls at a time should you cut from?

☐ a. One

☐ b. Two

☐ c. Three

5. True or False: When preparing to hang ceiling paper, you should measure the width of the ceiling and add an extra 80mm.

☐ a. True

☐ b. False

Chapter 6

END TEST

END TEST OBJECTIVES

The end test will check your knowledge on the information held within this workbook.

The Test

1. Which of the following options are some of the purposes for painting and decorating?

☐ a. Insulation

☐ b. Protection

☐ c. Sanitation

☐ d. Damp proofing

☐ e. Decoration

☐ f. Soundproofing

2. What are each of these tools used for? Match the pictures shown to the task descriptions.

Task	Tool
Lifting old wallpaper	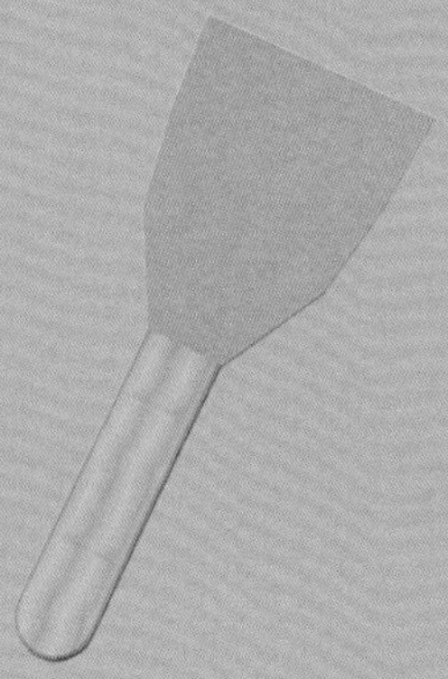

Task	Tool
Filling holes and cracks	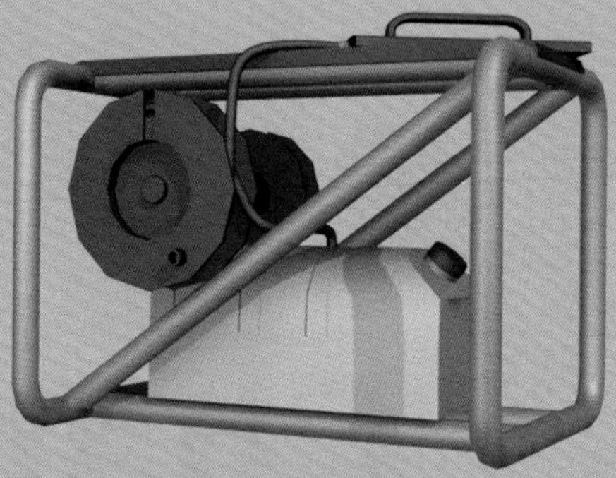
Removing old paint and wallpaper from flat surfaces	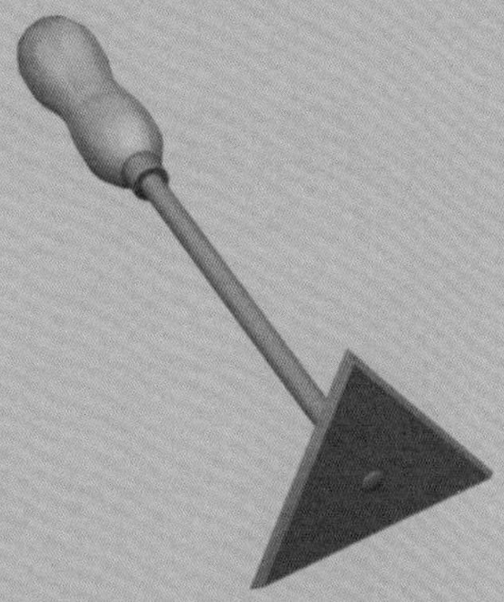
Removing old paint from mouldings and curved surfaces	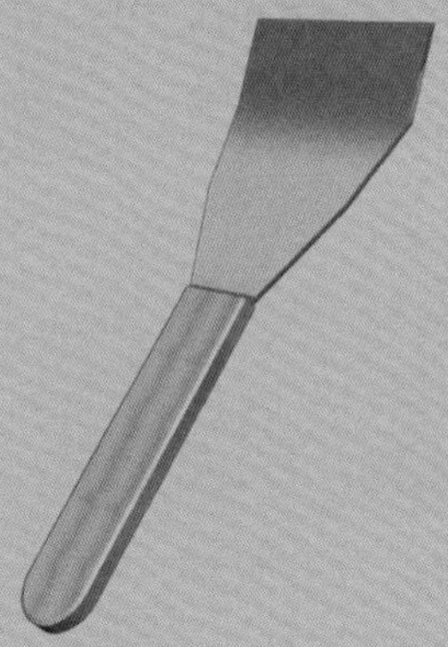

3. What are the different parts of a paintbrush called? Correctly label each part of the following picture.

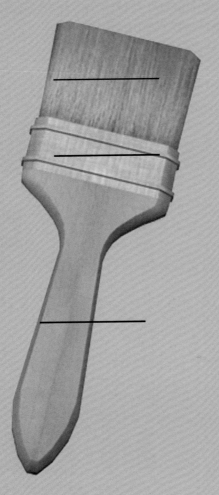

4. What size of paintbrush would you use for these jobs? Match the pictures shown to the task descriptions.

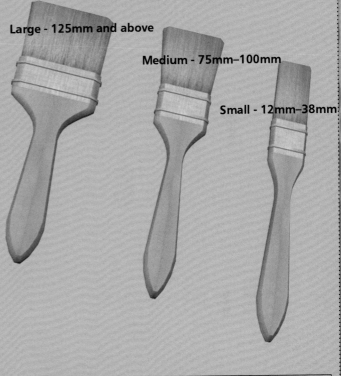

Large - 125mm and above

Medium - 75mm–100mm

Small - 12mm–38mm

Task	Brush size
Painting door panels	
Painting walls	
Cutting in	

5. Which of the following can the filling of paintbrushes be made from?

☐ a. Horse hair

☐ b. Wild boar bristles

☐ c. Nylon fibres

6. What are some of the purposes of lining paper?

☐ a. Providing decoration

☐ b. Providing an even surface

☐ c. Providing a surface with even porosity

☐ d. Soundproofing the surface

☐ e. Hiding irregularities

7. There are three different types of patterned papers shown here. Can you match them with the correct pattern names?

a. Random

b. Set

c. Drop match

8. Lining paper is hung horizontally when you are going to paper the surface.

☐ a. True

☐ b. False

9. Which of the following are methods for treating efflorescence?

☐ a. Replace damp surface

☐ b. Brush the surface

☐ c. Apply an acrylic

☐ d. Allow the surface to dry out

☐ e. Apply fungicide wash

10. What is the purpose of using a primer?

☐ a. Protects the surface

☐ b. Provides a key for other layers of paint to stick to

☐ c. Provides a smooth thick coat for other coats

☐ d. Gives a decorative finish

☐ e. Is absorbed into the surface to aid the application of other coats

11. What order should you follow to prepare an old plastered surface? Write your answers in the table below.

a. Clean surface

b. Repair damaged plaster

c. Sand down the plaster

d. Prime

e. Remove old paint and wallpaper

Step	Task
1	
2	
3	
4	
5	

12. The wallpaper batch number tells you the type of pattern the roll has.

☐ a. True

☐ b. False

13. What does this symbol mean?

☐ a. The paper has a set pattern

☐ b. The paper is ready pasted

☐ c. The paper has a random pattern

☐ d. Paste both sides

14. What order should you follow to paint a room? Write your answers in the table below.

a. Door

b. Walls

c. Ceiling

d. Skirting board

e. Window

f. Radiator

Step	Task
1	
2	
3	
4	
5	
6	

15. What adhesive should you use for these types of paper?

a. Cellulose adhesive

b. Vinyl adhesive

c. Starch-based paste

Paper	Adhesive
Vinyl paper	
Lightweight paper	
Medium weight paper	

16. You should use paint directly from the tin.

☐ a. True

☐ b. False

17. **What is the best practice order in which to paint a wall? Label the boxes 1 to 10.**

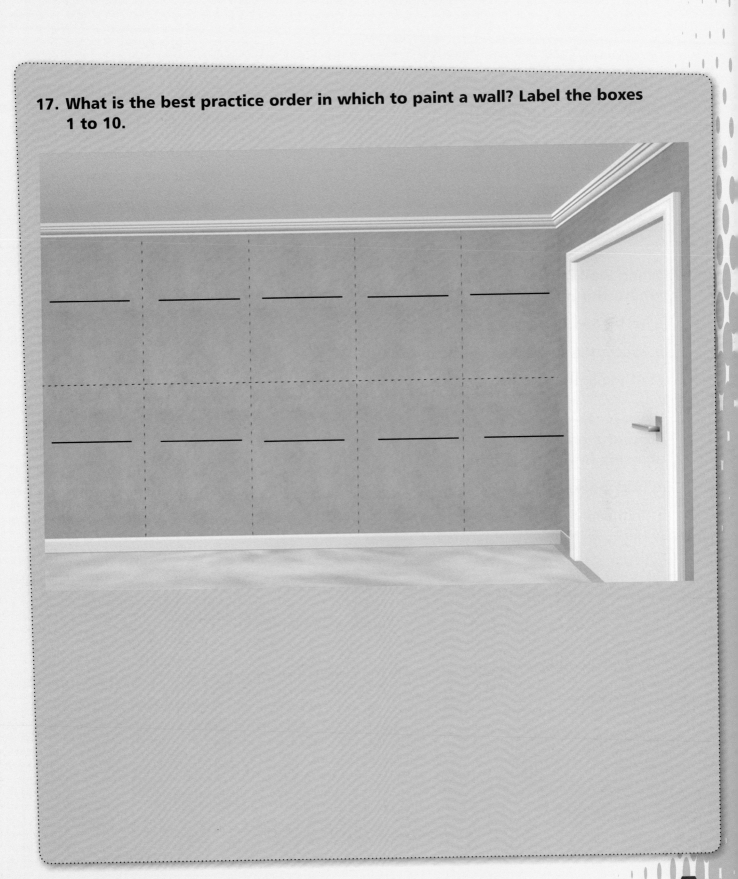

18. What is wet edge time?

☐ a. The time it takes for paint to dry

☐ b. The time you have until the paint you have just applied begins to dry off

☐ c. The time you have to wait to apply the next coat

19. When wallpapering a stairwell where should you start?

☐ a. At the top of the stairs

☐ b. Where the longest length will be

☐ c. At the bottom of the stairs

20. What is the process for pasting around a wall switch? Write your answers in the table below.

a. Find the corners

b. Trim paper

c. Tighten retaining screws

d. Undo switch retaining screws

e. Cut paper from centre to corners

f. Hang paper lightly over switch

g. Push the paper beneath switch

Step	Task
1	
2	
3	
4	
5	
6	
7	

Answers to Check Your Knowledge and End Test

CHAPTER 1

1. **B: False, the purposes of painting and decorating are protection, sanitation, conservation, identification and decoration.**

2. **C: You can train to be a painter and decorator at any age.**

3. **B: False, the painter and decorator will usually arrive towards the end of the project.**

CHAPTER 2

1.

Task	Tool
Removing paint from beading	

Task	Tool
Filling small holes	
Removing paint and wallpaper	
Abrading surfaces	

Task	Tool
Removing wallpaper ONLY	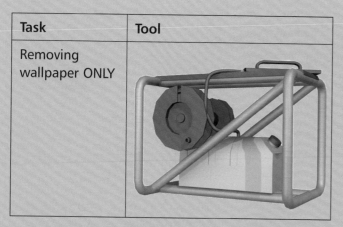

2. A, B and C: Paint includes binder, pigment and solvent.

3.

Symbol	Meaning
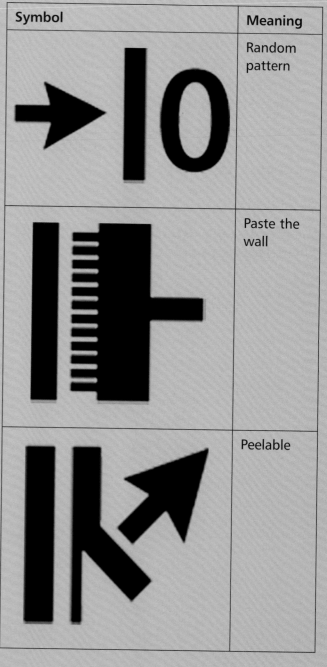	Scrubbable
	Paste the paper

Symbol	Meaning
	Random pattern
	Paste the wall
	Peelable

4. **A: True.**

5. **B: Clay based adhesives are coloured and tend to have the lowest water content (40–50 per cent).**

CHAPTER 3

1. **C: You should wait two weeks to allow the plaster to dry thoroughly.**

2. **D: The humidity level should not be above eighty per cent.**

3. **A: True.**

4. **B: False, softwood is made from coniferous trees such as pine, cedar or spruce.**

5. **A: Yes, you will need to remove badly flaking paint.**

CHAPTER 4

1. **A, B and E: Red, yellow and blue are the primary colours.**

2.

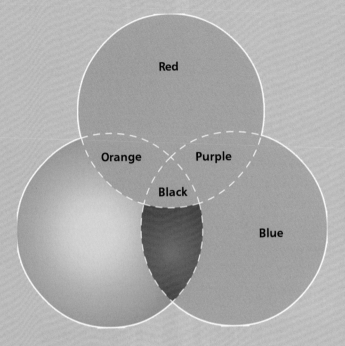

3. **A: True.**

4. **B: The ceiling should always be painted before the walls.**

CHAPTER 5

1. **A and C: The first length of paper could be hung either at the centre of the focal point of the room, or beside the source of natural light depending on the pattern of the paper.**

2. **A: Drop match.**

3. **B: The longest.**

4. B: You should cut from two rolls to match the pattern.

5. B: False, you should add an extra 40mm.

CHAPTER 6

Please check your answers against the following. If any of the questions you answered are incorrect you are advised to go back to that section in the workbook or the e-learning programme to re-study.

Question 1

B, C and E: The purposes for painting and decorating include protection, sanitation and decoration.

Question 2

Task	Tool
Lifting old wallpaper	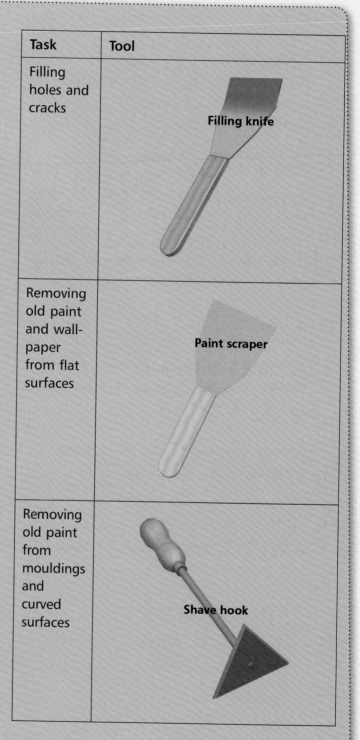Steam stripper
Filling holes and cracks	Filling knife
Removing old paint and wallpaper from flat surfaces	Paint scraper
Removing old paint from mouldings and curved surfaces	Shave hook

Question 3

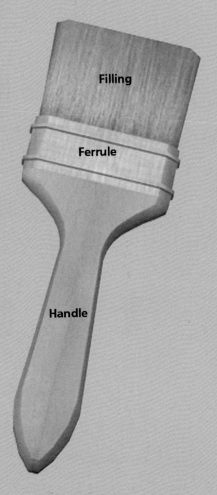

Filling

Ferrule

Handle

Question 4

Large – 125mm and above
Painting walls

Medium – 75mm–100mm
Painting door panels

Small – 12mm–38mm
Cutting in

Question 5

B and C: Paintbrush fillings can be made from natural materials such as wild boar bristles or man-made fibres such as nylon.

Question 6

B, C and E: Lining paper can be used to provide an even surface which hides irregularities and gives an even porosity.

Question 7

Drop match

Random match

Set

Question 8

True: Lining paper is hung horizontally for wallpapering and vertically for painting.

Question 9

A, B and D: You can treat efflorescence by brushing down the surface, replacing any damp surface and allowing the surface to dry fully.

Question 10

A, B and E: A primer can be used to aid the application of other coats, provide a key and protect the surface.

Question 11

Step	Task
1	Remove old paint and wallpaper
2	Repair damaged plaster
3	Sand down plaster
4	Clean surface
5	Prime

Question 12

False: The batch number will tell you that the rolls were created at the same time.

Question 13

A: The symbol means that the paper has a set pattern.

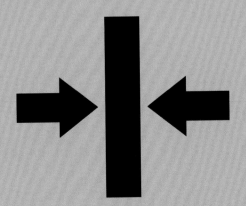

Question 14

Step	Task
1	Ceiling
2	Walls
3	Windows
4	Radiator
5	Skirting board
6	Door

Question 15

Paper	Adhesive
Vinyl paper	Vinyl adhesive
Lightweight paper	Cellulose adhesive
Medium weight paper	Starch-based paste

Question 16

False: You should not use paint directly from the tin. It is best practice to pour the paint into a separate container before using.

1	3	5	7	9
2	4	6	8	10

Question 18

B: The time you have until the paint you have just applied begins to dry off.

Question 19

B: You should start by first positioning the longest length then work up towards the landing, finishing with the downstairs.

Question 20

Step	Task
1	(D) Undo switch retaining screws
2	(F) Hang paper lightly over switch
3	(A) Find the corners
4	(E) Cut paper from centre to corners
5	(B) Trim paper
6	(G) Push the paper beneath switch
7	(C) Tighten retaining screws

Glossary

Abrade The wearing down of a particular material to make it suitable for the application of paint.

Adhesive General term given to a range of bonding agents.

Asbestos A fibrous mineral commonly used in buildings as fireproofing material until the mid-1980s. Can be a health hazard and should not be disturbed. Seek specialist advice if found or suspected.

Brickwork A solid wall built of bricks, laid to bond and in mortar. Used to be the most common load-bearing external wall construction. Mainly finished with fair faced bricks and pointed or rendered. Minimal maintenance required but as properties age partial or complete re-pointing or re-rendering respectively may become necessary.

Cavity The gap between the internal and external walls of a building. Usually 50mm wide to increase the thermal insulation and weather resistance of the wall. The cavity must be kept clear and not bridged (except for wall ties and insulation). A damp proof course (DPC) must be provided around the perimeter of openings in cavity walls otherwise dampness can occur internally.

Cement A grey or white powdery material made from chalk or limestone and clay. Cement is the most common binder in bricklaying mortar and works by hardening as a result of a chemical reaction when mixed with water. The most common type of cement is Ordinary Portland Cement (OPC).

Cill The sloping piece below a window for rainwater to run off.

Coalescence This process occurs when the water in paint evaporates. This leads to the molecules in the paint shrinking and sticking together to form a continuous film over the surface.

Coniferous tree A type of evergreen tree that produces its fruit in the form of cones.

Cornice A decorative moulding at the junction between the walls and ceiling of a room.

Corrosion The damage of a material by a substance such as rain or water.

Deciduous tree A tree that loses all of its leaves for part of the year.

Dust sheet A piece of material which protects household items from any spills, drips and dust during decorating.

Fungicide A chemical used to kill or slow down fungal decay on timber.

Hessian A natural-looking wallpaper that has a textured feel. It can be made from fabric or a woven material.

HSE Health and Safety Executive.

Ironmongery Products that have been manufactured from metal.

Lime There are two types of lime, hydraulic and non-hydraulic. They can both be used for mortar and pointing. The difference is in the setting time. The ratio for a lime mortar mix is six parts sand, one part lime and one part cement. Production and sustainability benefits make lime an eco-friendly material.

Lincrusta A deeply embossed wallcovering.

Mortar A mixture of sand, cement (sometimes with lime and/or additives) and water, used to bond stones and bricks. Can be mixed by hand or mechanically on- or off-site.

Muntin Vertical intermediate timbers between the panels of a door.

Paint kettle When painting, pour the paint into one of these to stop contamination of the manufacturer's paint tin.

Perimeter The border or outer boundary of an area.

Personal Protective Equipment (PPE) Depending on the type of work, there are different types of equipment specifically designed to protect your health and safety. Examples include gloves, safety boots, goggles and dust mask.

Plaster A white or pinkish mineral formed from heating gypsum at high temperatures. Plaster is used to protect and enhance the appearance of the surface as it provides a joint-less finish.

Plasterboard A type of board made of gypsum sandwiched between sheets of paper. It has a number of properties and can be made to different thicknesses and sizes for different areas and uses.

Plumb The vertical level of a surface or structure.

Plumb bob A weight attached to the plumb line, for checking vertical lines.

Plumb line Length of string with weight attached, for checking vertical lines.

Polymerization A process in painting where, as the paint dries, a series of chemical reactions occur which lead to the molecules in the paint bonding together to form a chain. These chains form a solid film of paint over the surface.

Prism A clear object which separates white light into a spectrum of different colours.

Render A sand and cement backing coat for tiling, usually applied in at least two coats.

Rendering The application of render to external wall surfaces for appearance or to make the wall waterproof. Crack may appear and should be repaired as progressively this will weather and lose key. allowing water to get behind render. This causes saturation of the wall which can result in fungal decay of structural timbers internally.

Resin A thick and sticky substance that is secreted by many plants especially deciduous trees.

Sand Fine aggregate that is one of the raw ingredients for mixing mortar.

Skirting A moulding covering the joint formed by a wall and the floor.

Spirit level A tool used to check true vertical and horizontal lines indicated by a bubble in spirit-filled vials.

Stile Upright framing of a door into which the ends of the horizontal rails are fixed.

Sustainable materials Materials that have been sourced by causing little or no damage to the environment.

Touch dry The stage during the drying of paint where it can be touched lightly without lifting any of the paint from the surface.

Veneer Very thin sheets of finely grained woods used to improve the aesthetics and strength of sheet materials e.g. blockboard.

Index